RESET

A.I.E.: ATTITUDE IS EVERYTHING

DHOMONIQUE MURPHY

New York | Los Angeles | London | Sydney

ISBN Softcover: 978-1-637921-20-3

TABLE OF CONTENTS

❖ Author's Note 6

❖ Testimonial 10

❖ Dedication 11

❖ Part 1: Own Your 'Reset' 13

   ° Goals Aspirations: A Mental Paradigm Shift 15

   ° Self-Defined: You Shape Your Reality 26

   ° Self-Care: The Power of Your Thoughts 46

   ° Holistic Being: Health, Wealth, Spirituality, ... 53
     and Gratitude

❖ Part 2: Reset Your Attitude 69

   ° How To Use This System 71

   ° 30-Day Guided Self-Reset System 73

   ° Congratulations! You're Living Your Best Life 172

❖ References 174

❖ About the Author 175

AUTHOR'S NOTE

Dear Aspirer,

Since the outbreak of COVID-19, we have all experienced our fair share of delays, uncertainty, disappointment, and losses. To navigate unexpected scenarios and manage unforeseen obstacles, many of our goals have been postponed or even cancelled. As you look to the future and a post- COVID-19 world, you might be wondering where those lofty goals you had fit into the big picture now, and whether you can get back on track.

If so, I want to encourage you that it is still possible to live your best life and achieve your aspirations. While a post-COIVD-19 world environment is, indeed, a whole new ballgame, it's still very possible for you to monetize your unique set of skills, attributes, and passions. It is still possible to live your best life after COVID-19. While your goals may be have been delayed, your aspirations and potential are as strong as ever. You can still realize your vision, fulfill your aspirations, build wealth, and achieve the success you desire.

It all boils down to your mindset, your willingness to act, and your ability to accept risk in pursuit of opportunity. Rather than labeling your next move as "getting back on track", think of it as a reset on your life. An opportunity to wipe the slate clean and start anew. It sounds magical, doesn't it? I want to encourage you that it's within your power to do so – to own your reset. The first step in this process is to connect (or reconnect) with your purpose.

Finding Your Anchor

In the midst of the most vicious storm, it's the anchor that keeps the ship grounded. Knowing your why is one of the most – if not *the* most – important steps towards changing your life for the better. Your why is your anchor. When a storm comes your way (like the unforeseen crisis we are living through today), the power of your purpose will give you determination and courage you never knew you had. Having a clear sense of purpose enables you to focus your efforts on what matters most, set yourself up for opportunities, push forward regardless of the obstacles, and compel you to take risks.

As you begin your journey of living your best life, I challenge you to take a moment to ask yourself a few important questions: "What is my 'why'?" "What is my driving force behind building wealth and improving my wellbeing?" "What would my life look like tomorrow if I pursue financial and emotional freedom today?"

Enjoying the Benefits

While resetting will look different for everyone, the end goal is the same. Freedom. In mastering certain aspects of your life – health, wealth, spirituality, and gratitude – you will experience true freedom in your life. Your aspirations will be more attainable. You will achieve a greater sense of wholeness. Ultimately, creating financial and emotional freedom allows you to:

> ➤ Make decisions based on long-term goals, not immediate survival. The economic slump caused by COVID-19 will

not be the last crisis or obstacle we face. Building wealth will allow you to not only gain control over your day-to-day life, but also insulate your finances for whatever the future may hold.

➤ Focus on what you *want* to do, not what you *have* to do. The greater the financial and emotional burden you carry, the more your life will revolve around doing what you have to do to get by. When you build up true wealth, you will be free (financially and emotionally) to set your life up to enjoy more of what you love each day.

➤ Align your actions with your values. When you are stuck in a cycle of debt and uncertainty, it's not uncommon to find yourself sacrificing what is most important to you to make ends meet. Resetting your mind and building up financial stability ensures your money is being used in way that demonstrates and supports your values.

➤ Gain a new perspective on your future. With the freedom that comes from shifting your mindset, your dreams will no longer be some far-off vision. You will not only be able to enjoy life's little moments, but also achieve success and create a lifestyle beyond your wildest dreams. The sky is literally the limit!

➤ Enjoy financial peace and better health. The age-old saying, "health is wealth," is more than just a cliché; there really are connections between the state of your finances and your health, with symptoms that go far beyond stress. As you reset and build a strong foundation, you will also discover a greater sense of emotional peace and live an all-around healthier life.

➤ Be better prepared to accept risks in order to chase opportunity. It's only natural to become risk-averse in the wake of a crisis like COVID-19. However, the secret to recovery is to take bold action and embrace risks that spur growth. Building a solid foundation will give you the confidence you need to accept some risks and the wisdom to evaluate the potential reward.

The Journey Begins

So, is it really possible for you to come out of this crisis in a better place than you started? The answer is yes! A big resounding yes! Learning how to reset yourself and adapt your mindset is the secret to continuing to achieve your aspirations in life, regardless of the crisis or situation you face.

Through this book, I hope to uplift and inspire you to see any shaky event that takes place in your life as an opportunity to reset. My hope is that the information within these pages will help you unlock the power of your purpose and live your best life. It's time to start the journey of discovering your potential and building the wealth and prosperity you and your loved ones so deserve.

"Dhomonique is one of the most inspiring and most helpful people that you will ever work with, and if you follow her ideas over and over again, you will accomplish more in the weeks and months ahead then you may have ever accomplished in your whole lifetime."
– Brian Tracy

"You gotta follow her. Stay close to her and see everything that she does because it's transformational."
– Mitch Axelrod
#1 Bestselling Author, Speaker, Strategist-IP

"Dhomonique is The World's Most Inspiring and Gifted Interviewer."
– Mitzi Perdue
Speaker and World Thought-Leader

This book is dedicated to my amazing husband and best friend, Frank, and our two brilliant baby boys, Christian and Christopher. May you two always know that you can accomplish anything you set your minds to.

This book is also dedicated to YOU. You now have me in your corner. Consider me a friend and an advocate for YOU. It's time for you to take control of your life, and I am going to help you do it—and WIN.

Part 1

OWN YOUR 'RESET'

~~GOALS~~ ASPIRATIONS
A Mental Paradigm Shift

"To understand the heart and mind of a person, look not at what he has already achieved, but at what he aspires to." – Khalil Gibran

Goals and Aspirations

When I was 14 years old, I didn't have a goal written down on how I could and would eventually get into the media and television industry. I *aspired* to be on television. Aspirations don't change the way goals do. Aspirations are a part of our *identity*; whereas, a goal is merely a grounded plan of action on a desired outcome. Consider this: how many people do you know who have earned a degree they don't really use? Or have a talent they have no interest in capitalizing?

Earning a degree obviously requires that one make and achieve an established goal, however their degree may actually be completely independent of their aspiration in life. Likewise, a talent can help one to achieve many goals in life, but that does not automatically mean that their talent is their aspiration. Just because you may be able to sing well does not mean you aspire to be a singer; however, you may still achieve singing goals, such as learning a new vocal technique or performing at a recital, despite the fact that you *aspire* to be something else. It is very possible that your goals may have **nothing** to do with your aspirations.

I remember watching a video clip of Bishop T. D. Jakes recounting a conversation he had with his eldest son, who was preparing for college at the time. His son was worried that his choice of major wouldn't be "the thing" God called him to do. Bishop Jakes encouraged him to pursue the degree anyway, "… because even if it wasn't the thing, it would be the thing that *leads to* the thing." Sometimes goals *lead* to aspirations. Bishop Jakes gives us another understanding of goals versus aspirations. It may take a goal—or even a series of goals—to reach one's aspiration in life.

Many of our goals may have been interrupted by the global pandemic, COVID-19. A novel virus has forced the entire world to come to a screeching halt. A life that was once unthinkable is now mandatory. So many of our norms have been stripped away from us. And griefs that are already hard have been made even harder to bear by this virus. As difficult as these experiences can be, I want to encourage you and let you know that though your goals may have been cancelled, your aspirations are never cancelled. This is why it is *still possible* to live your best life after COVID-19.

I want to speak to what you aspire to be. I want to encourage and uplift who you aspire to be. I want to share my experiences and my methods with you, and hopefully, share some of the joy I have found in living my best life, despite my own setbacks and losses.

Paradigm Shift

However, in order for me to discover how to live my best life despite my own goals being deterred or destroyed, I had to change the way that I saw my life's purpose. As simple as this may seem, this was one of the most profound and difficult decisions that I ever had to make. It was difficult in the sense that although it was easy for my mind to understand, it took much longer for my heart to catch up. Personally, my paradigm shift was not an overnight victory. To be completely honest, it was emotionally exhausting, challenging, and humbling. Nevertheless, I wouldn't trade my experience for any other, and it is my hope and belief that the same will be your testimony at the end of your paradigm shift.

What exactly is a "paradigm shift"? In 1962, physicist and philosopher Thomas Kuhn coined the term "paradigm shift" in his influential book, *"The Structure of Scientific Revolutions"* (Kuhn, 1996). Essentially, Kuhn was explaining how emerging information could change the way people saw and interpreted natural sciences—this principle is what he referred to as a *paradigm shift*. He demonstrated this principle using the famous duck-rabbit optical illusion, to show how a paradigm shift could cause one to see the same information in a different way (Kuhn, 1996). Even though Kuhn was only referring to scientific information, the term "paradigm shift" has since been applied to many non-scientific contexts (Kuhn, 1996).

Duck-Rabbit Optical Illusion, made famous by Ludwig Wittgenstein in 1892

A.I.E.: Attitude is Everything

I believe that a paradigm shift in the way one sees their life purpose and meaning—or their aspirations—is crucial to owning his or her 'reset'. Essentially, A.I.E.: Attitude is everything. As you look at the picture above, if you perceive the animal is facing *left*, you will see the "duck"; however, if you perceive the animal is facing *right*, you will see the "rabbit". Get this: a simple adjustment in which way you perceive the animal is facing changed its species, name, *and* its direction! All of a sudden, a bird that was flying west became a mammal that was hopping on paws eastward. Now, imagine if we made a simple adjustment in the way we saw the direction of our life, what would it become?

Let's use "Jane" as an example: Jane sings very well, but she does not aspire to be a singer, but, rather, she aspires to be in engineering. On one hand, Jane sings so well that she has become a lead vocalist in her local band. On the other hand, Jane is earning her doctoral degree online to further her career in engineering, and hopefully land the job of her dreams. The extra money she makes from singing engagements is only enough to cover some of her educational expenses. Singing makes Jane happy, but engineering makes Jane **shine** on the inside. However, tragedy strikes and swipes Jane's opportunity away when COVID-19 shuts down the company she really wanted a job in. In addition, Jane can only perform online shows now and doesn't make nearly as much money as she used to. Now, Jane feels jaded. She feels as though she will live the rest of her year(s), miserable, behind in her bills, and struggling to make ends meet. With this perspective of her life, Jane can only see the animal facing *left*; she can only see the "duck." How can one simple adjustment turn Jade's entire life around? Let's continue to hear more of her story.

Reset

Jane's friend shared a YouTube video with her one day. It was a clip of a motivational speaker talking about making a personal paradigm shift. The speaker said, "The only reason it's the end for you is because you *believe* it is. That's the verdict you gave it." Jane paused the video immediately. She just sat there for a few minutes and pondered on the speaker's words. Eventually, Jane came to the conclusion that the speaker was absolutely right. After a few minutes, Jane thought to herself, "So, what if I actually believed that it was not the end for me? What would happen if I decided that my life was not over yet?"

Then, Jane put down her tablet and made a difficult call. Jane called her younger sister—a mother of two—for some financial assistance until she was able to get caught back up. Jane made an arrangement to pay her sister back after she had gotten all caught up in her bills. Jane reached out to two of her professors and asked them for extra credit and assistance to help her pick her grades back up, as depression had interrupted her pristine academic performance. Jane was open with her professors and explained her situation and why she had fallen behind. To her surprise, one of her professors was able to work with some of the university staff to help pull some special strings for Jane. Jane was offered a paid internship at a local engineering facility where theme park parts were designed, created, and distributed nationwide. At the end of the internship, provided that Jane graduated with a high grade point average, Jane would be offered the position at full-time with benefits. It wasn't the job that she dreamed of, but it was more than enough to get her through her current situation.

Now, Jane could see the animal facing to the *right*; now, she could see the "rabbit." However, she didn't see the rabbit only after she was offered the internship; Jane actually saw the rabbit when she decided to pick up her phone and call her sister. That was the moment. That was the crucial moment in time that turned Jane's life completely around. This is the very reason why paradigm shifts are much easier said than done. It is so hard, and it takes much longer than we anticipate, often because we don't realize that we have seen a light at the end of the tunnel until after we made the decision that seems to be the hardest. We can only imagine how Jane was embarrassed to ask her little sister for financial assistance. Jane had to lay her pride aside and make a decision that did not provide her the luxury of "saving face". In that moment, Jane still could not see the light at the end of the tunnel; Jane had not yet realized that she had finally seen the "rabbit". In her mind, all she was doing was "the next right thing". I called that moment Jane's **"reset"** moment. Before we get any further, I want to make sure you understand what I mean by *owning your reset*.

Resetting is relative; it looks different for everyone. For one person, it could simply mean trying again. For another person, it could mean stopping everything, wiping the slate clean, and starting all over. It could mean taking a risk; it could mean taking a break. However, to achieve this paradigm shift in your mind, it's about more than just taking the risk or starting all over. You have to *own* that. But what does that really mean? Simply put, when you own something, your name is on that deed. In legal terms, you are solely responsible for it. You are also responsible for delegating authority to someone else if, for any reason, you are unable to take care of it.

I am pretty sure we can all agree that owning a car feels a lot different than owning a demotion; even owning a phone feels much different than owning a lay-off. Think about that for a moment. If someone had a car that was stolen, they would be responsible for picking it up when it was found, and also taking care of it, regardless of whether or not they were compensated for damages. However, imagine someone having to own a demotion in the same way. Let's say a veteran officer was demoted to desk duty until further notice, due to recklessness on the job. The officer is not only responsible to his department for his actions, but also to the other party who was affected, and he is even responsible to his own family for the strain that it may force on them.

Ownership, per se, is nebulous; it is *what* we own and the way we handle it that truly matters. The owner of the car may have mismanaged her finances, instead of making the sacrifices necessary to take care of her vehicle; whereas the veteran officer may have issued a genuine apology to his department, to the party that he affected, and to his family, while getting another side job to compensate for the money loss until he was able to stabilize again. It doesn't matter what we own as much as how we *handle* what we own. So, when I say, "own your reset," I mean that no matter how hard the next right thing is, can you reset yourself the best way you can—even knowing things may still not turn out the way you expected?

Even if your honest answer to that question is "I'm not sure"—or even "Nah, fam"—I am *still* here to tell you, that it's okay. This book is to serve as a guide to help you find your 'next right thing,' reset your mind and tame your thoughts, and live your best life, despite the blows that COVID-19 may have forced on you. So far, we learned how to identify our aspiration by seeing the direction of our life in a different way. Now that we have our aspiration, we have our finish line, or where we hope to be at the end of 30 days. Write down your aspiration after this prompt: I **aspire** to...

_____

_____

_____

However, we need a new starting line: this is our **reset**. Creating a fresh starting place for ourselves can help us find our new center of gravity, especially after a paradigm-shifting event such as COVID-19. So, now, it's time to answer perhaps the hardest question you will read throughout this book: right now, what is your next right thing? The next right thing may not *always* be the decision that gets you what you want, but rather gets you what you need or even *where* you need to be. The closer you get to where you need to be, the more you are ***progressing*** toward your reset; however, the further you are getting from where you need to be, the more you are *regressing* from your reset. A **progression** is when you handle or respond to a situation with better skills, decisions, and/or a better attitude than you might have otherwise responded in previous times. Remember "A.I.E.": Attitude is *everything*. A **regression** is when you revert back to a more primitive mental and/or emotional way after you have made a progression in that same part of yourself. Now, write down your reset after this prompt: I acknowledge that I am where I am and that I cannot change what has already happened, therefore, I choose to reset myself by…

_____

_____

_____

Now, look at your starting line directly above this sentence. Then, look at your finish line that you wrote first. The reason why I asked you to write it down in that order, is because I wanted you to have this visual in your mind. Living your best life is going to require that you move from this *bottom* sentence to the **top** sentence—that is, you are about to begin your journey, and you are going to go from the bottom to the top. 30 days from today, (*write today's date down, too*) _____, you will be living your best life after COVID-19. Now, that means that your best life may not look like what you originally expected it to be, but it will lead you to something that will be even better than anything you ever imagined. In Bishop Jakes's words, "it may not be the thing, but it will be the thing that *leads to* the thing". Remember Jane's story? In the same way, it may not be your ideal choice, but it may certainly lead you to something you never dreamed or hoped for! Are you ready? Yes? Okay. I will make a deal with you...

Literally. I want you to print and sign below next to my name and signature, that according to the date and terms you have written above, **you** will hereby commit to making your best life a reality, using my book as your guide. I believe in you. I expect the best from you. And I am rooting and cheering for you all the way!

<u>**Dhomonique Ricks**</u>   _____

My Name, Printed   *Your Name, Printed*

_____   _____

My Signature   *Your Signature*

Breathe

Ironically, one of the vocal techniques Jane learned how to use was called "aspiration". To *aspirate* while singing means to use an audible puff of *breath*, in order to help the singer inflect note or key changes. For example, in the national anthem, the line that says "o'er the laaa-and of the free..." will actually sound like "o'er the laaa-**hand** of the free", since "land" is two notes, and not just one. In Classical Latin, the root word *pira* means "breath." Why am I telling you this?

I want to let you in on a secret. Not only is there power in your thoughts, but there is tremendous power in your <u>words</u>. If we analogize our thoughts with seeds, then our words are like the water that nourishes and feeds those seeds. This is why saying a daily affirmation to yourself is so powerful. But in this book, #**AOTD** means *aspiration of the day*. Whether you only have one aspiration in life or ten, it does not matter. As you go through this book every day in the journal section, I want you to start by writing your daily aspiration.

Every time you affirm your aspiration to yourself, it's like taking in a *breath of fresh air to your mind*. When you stop affirming these aspirations to yourself, it's like trying to sing without taking in enough air first. Any vocalist will tell you that if you try to sing without first having air to support the note, your voice will crack. Trying to force your body to work without enough air may cause you to faint. Every time you recite your daily aspiration(s), I want to say it out loud to yourself, *while* looking in the mirror, **and** making eye contact with yourself. When you do this, you are equipping your mind with the *pira* or the breath that it needs to be able to reset without growing faint throughout the process.

SELF-DEFINED
You Shape Your Reality

"You don't become what you want…
you become what you believe."

– Oprah Winfrey

"Good" Advice

I want to share a story with you about a moment in my life that changed me forever. It is interesting that when we see the word "**self-defined**", we automatically think of ourselves—*by* ourselves. But being self-defined does not imply that you, alone, contribute to who you turn out to be. The words, thoughts, and actions of others can change your perspective, and make you reconsider how you see yourself or how you want others to see you. And you can do all of this without invalidating who you are: you are simply defining yourself.

I was in college at the University of Missouri. It was my junior year, and I had finally made it into the J-School (Journalism School). All students were required to take a class from a teacher who was famous for being extra tough. Our first assignment was to fill out a biography form and attach a picture to it. On the first day of class, this teacher walked in front of each student, read their paper out loud, and then asked them a few questions. I was sitting in the middle of the room. It was a crisp fall day. I still remember the brown metallic bubble vest I was wearing. The teacher got to my desk, and I handed him my sheet of paper and nervously waited. He started at it longer than anyone else he had already stopped in front of. Then he looked up at me and said, "Who's *this*?" referring to the image on my form. I swallowed hard and sank down into my seat.

I answered, "That's me." "Doesn't look like you," he grumbled and then asked me, "Where are you from?" "MinnesOOOOta," I replied. Then he said, in front of the entire classroom, "If you ever want to get a job in television outside of Minnesota, you've got to lose that accent." The class started laughing, and I was mortified. Although the message was hard to hear, he was right. Sometimes, the best words of advice may be presented in ways that are not the most appropriate. I took that sound advice and made it my mission to drop my deep-rooted Minnesota accent. I was able to accomplish that, and it led me to lead a very successful journalism and public speaking career.

It's moments like these that shape us and mold our character and strengthen our fortitude. In the end, we decide what we want to be and how; however, it is our experiences with others that lead us to those life-changing moments. Define who you are, but remember to include the considerations of others, even if they don't come across the best way.

Self Made

At the end of the limited series *Self Made*, featuring award-winning actress Octavia Spencer, one's heart is left carrying the weight of how hard a self-made life can really be. However, a self-made man or woman must first be self-defined. Usually, when someone asks you, "Who are you," you give them your name and title. But as I ask you this question, I don't want you to answer with your name. Answer with your aspiration. Who are you... *really?* It's okay if you don't have an answer right at this moment, however, this is part of your paradigm shift, which will help you own your 'reset'.

Right now, if we were to survey a lot of self-made successful people, we would be able to quickly assess that self-made persons *made* themselves. Per the previous section, I do not mean that they got where they were in life *by* themselves, but rather, I mean that they decided to achieve their aspirations by themselves. I can almost guarantee you that there was a point in every one of their lives where they had to make a decision within themselves without the assistance of anybody else that they were going to achieve their aspiration in life. You, too, have to have this "self-made" moment. Whatever it is that you aspire to do or be, you have to make the choice to achieve it.

I don't mean to have the idea passively sitting loftily in your mind, as something you occasionally daydream about from time to time. I mean you have to actively pursue it every single day. You have to actively pursue it today, regardless of whether you succeed or fail. Tomorrow, when you wake up, you have to actively pursue it, regardless of how much progress you made today. The day after tomorrow, you have to wake up and pursue it, regardless of how tired you might be of it. The day after that, you have to wake up and pursue it, without allowing competing demands to drown out that light inside you.

For some of you, this may be second nature. However, for some of you, this mindset may be easily exhausting. You might be able to pick it up for one day, two days, maybe even three days. But then after that, something else gets your full attention, and you devote your energy toward that, leaving your aspirations to collect dust on the back burner. This is why I always say "A.I.E.": Attitude is everything.

Now, it doesn't mean or speak to anything about your level of determination or your drive. It just simply means that you handle your aspirations in a different way. We will explore more about this in the "Holistic Being" section, but just because you handle your aspirations differently, doesn't mean that you have to sacrifice active, consistent pursuit of your aspirations for a new approach.

Simply put, being self-made is hard work. It is hard work all the time. And this is not the kind of hard work that gets easier once you attain that aspiration; rather, this is the kind of hard work that actually escalates, or at least maintains, once you achieve whatever your aspiration is. If you have a harder time with long-term goals, you have to understand that your aspiration is not a goal at all, or a chore. We do not regard daily activities such as bathing, eating, and sleeping as chores. These are things we have done all of our lives and will continue to do for the rest of our lives.

We will alter our patterns of these based on our needs, or even our aspirations. For example, if our aspiration calls for a higher level of productivity, we may reduce our sleeping pattern and increase our eating pattern to keep us motivated and energized. However, if we have an aspiration that calls for a higher level of focus, we may increase our sleeping pattern and decrease or put restrictions on our eating pattern to keep our minds sharp and alert. Once we approach our aspirations as a need, rather than a chore, it becomes easier to approach and accept all of the hard, self-made work it will require to achieve our aspirations. It will make adjustments in our mindset easier, and it will make exercises, such as the ones in this book, have more meaning and value to us. The more meaning and value we add to our aspirations, the more we will be able to override the systems in our mind that tell us that we can relax on or put off our aspirations.

This is why the need of taking out the trash on a regular basis overrides how heavy the bag may be or how smelly it may be to carry it outside; to avoid any hazards or discomfort in your home, you will go through the ritual of taking out the trash on a frequent basis. Now, I wouldn't compare reaching your aspirations to taking out the trash, but the same diligence and consistency it requires to maintain your home safety and comfort is required in order to achieve your aspirations in life. It may not be on a daily basis, but on a consistent basis you have to revisit your aspirations and recharge so that you can pursue it actively in your life. This is what a self-made life looks like.

Finally, being self-made requires that you define your own aspirations. If I define your aspirations, it may be possible for a few of you, but it would be nearly impossible for the rest of you. Even if I were to give you a dictionary definition of aspiration, only some would be able to achieve it; others might still feel it was impossible to implement in their lives. But if *you* define your own aspirations, it will be most likely that you will attain it. Over the next four sections, we are going to define different dimensions of our aspirations for ourselves, so that we can holistically achieve our aspirations.

Health

Health is something that is so important to me. I would like to share a personal experience where I jeopardized my own health because of the opinions of others. Health is such a personal thing. I follow my doctor's advice and I exercise regularly, however, what works for one may not work best for another.

During my time in Lynchburg, Virginia, I decided I was going to run for Miss Virginia USA. I had worked out a deal with my television station to allow me to do this. I had run in the qualifiers for Miss Minnesota America a few years prior and lost and decided this time, I was going to go all in. I was determined to win this time, and I was not going to let anything stop me. I went all in and trained for 12 months to make my dream a reality. I pulled all my money out of my accounts and decided I was going to invest it all on building my brand via the pageant world. I had a pageant coach, a trainer, a dietitian, a wardrobe stylist, a hair stylist, even a custom-made dress. I trained harder than I ever had in my life, but guess what happens when you rely on several people telling you what *they* think you need to do without any insight from you? You lose your identity. You lose your voice. You lose your authenticity. That's what happened to me.

I was listening to so many outside voices telling me what I needed to look like, how to dress, what to wear, that Dhomonique was lost in all of it. What did *I* want, need, and desire? It was unclear. In the end, the pageant arrived, and it instantly became crystal clear that even though I "prepared" for an entire year, I was not prepared at all. I had lost too much weight; I was frail. My extensions were way too thin, and my styling was not competition-ready, and my dress didn't fit! I made it to the semi-final round, but then was eliminated. I was devastated.

I had invested 12 months into training like my life depended on it. I had spent thousands and thousands of dollars. I always made myself a promise that would return to the stage and earn a title at some point in my life. My time was going to come. I held on to that vision and never lost sight of it. I put it in my pocket and held it close. I didn't compete for nearly a decade. Nine years later, it was my time. I was ready and this was now my time. But this time, I was doing it *my* way. I knew what I wanted, how I wanted to look and feel, and I had a clear understanding of my "why" and my passions. I am so grateful to say, I am Mrs. Virginia American 2020, but more importantly, I am truly me!

To me, health is way more than just body mass index and calorie counts. Health is your mindset, your voice, your identity, and your happiness. Without those things, I believe the heart gets sick, and to be sick emotionally or mentally can be just as damaging as physical sickness.

Let's shift gears and do a brief exercise. Upon the following prompt below, I want you to write down the first three things that come to mind.

Healthy

_____

_____

_____

Now, it would be easy to say that what you've written above is your definition of "healthy". However, your definition is actually "hidden" in your mind somewhere beneath these three words. To define something yourself is to create something, or to shape something— I dare say, even *invent* something. Let's think about this from the perspective of invention. When someone invents something, normally, they don't take absolutely nothing and just produce any old thing. They take the things and/or people that they already know around them and produce something that can work with/for them.

Let's say that the three things you wrote above are the things that you already know. What is something that you could invent or create that could work for or with those things in regards to your health? For example, let's say that I wrote down "free of illness", "alert", and "happy". I want to invent something that can work for and or with these things. So, I don't want my definition of health to be something like "family", because family can sometimes pass on germs. And I don't want my definition to be something like "employment", because I may move, and my job may change, and it may not make me completely happy. My definition of health is something that facilitates all three of these, always. Therefore, here is an example of my self-definition of health: *My health is my good hygiene and nutrition habits.* Even if I were to fall ill—God forbid—practicing good nutrition and hygiene helps me heal, keeps me alert, and makes me happy.

Now, look back at your three things, and write your definition of health below:

_____

_____

_____

The definition that you have written above for yourself is a principle that you want to live by as you continue to achieve your aspirations. This definition will help you to focus on and steer yourself back toward your aspiration if you ever lose focus. So, bookmark this page for reference, so that you can always look back and remind yourself what health looks like to you and stay on track.

Wealth

Again, after the prompt below, I want you to write down the first three things that come to mind.

Wealthy

_____

_____

_____

This is so crucial and important that you define wealth for yourself. We do not do this as often with our health as we do with wealth: it is easier for us to follow after the trends of another's wealth, especially when we see that it's working for them so much better than ours seems to be working for us. However, you wouldn't blindly follow someone else's health regimen in order to get results similar to theirs, would you? It may seem that the results will manifest for you the same way that it did for them, but the reality is you actually don't know that. It could be something genetically or biologically different in you that may alter the results for you. Additionally, you don't know if you can follow the same health regimen as rigorously or intensely as the other person did, without risking the safety of your own health.

I want to submit for your consideration the same concept for your wealth, as with your health. It is not always the safest idea to blindly follow after someone else's idea of wealth, simply because you do not know all of the factors that their personal wealth system entails. Doing this may risk the safety of your own wealth. Even if you and your neighbor wrote down the same three things in your books for wealth, their definition of wealth can still manifest differently for them than it came for you, simply because you two are not the same person.

Now, remember: you want to make your definition of wealth something that can facilitate all three things that you've written down, regardless of the situation. Review your three things again, and write down your definition of wealth below:

_____

_____

_____

Spirituality

Although I am not going to define spirituality for you, I would like to share with you what spirituality is *not*. Spirit comes from the Hebrew word "*rûach*", which means "wind". If you will allow me to digress, wind is one of the four main natural elements, including water, fire, and earth. Water revives or nourishes things. Fire destroys or resets things. Earth grows or creates things. But wind *moves* things, or repositions them. Think of your spirit as a kind of **transporter**. A transporter takes something of use and relocates it to a place where it can be optimized. So, let's say that you have a brilliant idea. Your spirit's job is to transport this brilliant idea from inside your mind to outside you, where it can be optimized.

Now of course, the first thing you may notice about this is that moving something from inside your mind to an external environment is not something that can be defined in concrete or even logical terms. It seems like more of a far-fetched goal or an abstract idea. If you are practical and structured, this may not be as second nature to you as it is for someone who is a visionary; in fact, it may frustrate you. However, as I've mentioned before, this has nothing to do with your level of drive, but it simply means that you handle your aspirations in other way.

Returning to my original point, now that we understand the basic function of spirituality, let us review some things that spirit is **not**. The spirit is not a religion. Your spirit may *use* religion in order to do its job, but it is not, in and of itself, a religion. The spirit is not a culture. Similar to religion, your spirit may use your culture in order to do its job, but it is not a culture. For instance, you may be so inspired by your culture that you become an advocate. What your spirit has done is it has used your culture as a facilitator to transport your aspiration of being an advocate from inside your mind to externally, where your gift of advocacy can be optimized. Finally, the spirit is not a deity or a body. Sometimes, it may be harder to connect with anything invisible or intangible, but our spirit has more to do with who we are than it has to do with what we are made of. Similarly, our spirit has more to do with who we know than who we follow. To move our ideals from within us to without us, our spirit may use the deities that we follow and the bodies that we have to do so, but *our spirit* is distinctive from either.

Knowing this, write down the first three things that come to mind after the prompt below:

Spirituality

_____

_____

_____

Now, create your own definition of spirituality, which should be able to work with all three of the things that you've written above:

_____

_____

_____

Gratitude

Of the four aspects of a self-made life, gratitude seems like the least relative. At first glance, it may not seem that gratitude has anything to do with achieving your aspirations. If you want anything in life, you simply go after it, right? What about ambition necessitates being thankful? Well, allow me to answer a question with a scenario. You have two employees. Both employees' performance is high-level and equally impressive. Both are eligible for the same promotion. Literally the only thing that distinguishes their performance is their names. However, their presence is clearly distinguishable. You can tell this because one employee clocks in and clocks out, and just provides excellent service. Meanwhile, the other employee shows gratitude for every opportunity. This employee says thank you for praise, criticism, and welcomes suggestions from customers. Which one are you more inclined to give the promotion to? Let's not make this about work. Let's say we have two children. They both behave very well, but one child goes out of their way to show gratitude to the other students, as well as the teacher. Which one are you more inclined to give a reward?

Gratitude is one of those little pebbles that can crack an entire window. Compared to the other dimensions of being, it does not match in size, but the impact it can make affects the outcome. In this 30-day reset system, the purpose of gratitude is not so much to fuel you along the way, but rather to significantly increase your projected outcome. Reviewing both of the scenarios above, we can see how little drops of gratitude can actually make a difference in the outcome, especially when your odds are level with the odds of a competitor. It's true: when we show gratitude toward others, it alters the outcome of their evaluation or judgment of us. Those who show gratitude tend to score higher on their evaluations and on their presentations, because sometimes, it's more than just about the work you put in, but it's also about the *way* that you put in your work. So, if gratitude can have this effect on others when we show it toward them, imagine the impact that gratitude can have on us when we show it toward *ourselves*.

So, when you ask yourself, "What am I grateful for," it's great to be thankful for the things that friends do for us and the things that family does for us, especially when they don't have to. But it's so important to focus on what you are grateful for within *yourself*. I want to be careful to highlight this, because I want you to remember that the entire point of the system is to work on resetting *yourself*, defining *yourself*, and living *your* best life.

Now, this doesn't negate the gratitude of others at all. In fact, I'd like to share with you one of the people that I am most grateful for in my life. Aside from my wonderful husband and my two amazing boys, I am grateful to that manager who demoted me…11 days before my wedding! Yep! That's right! What that manager did was the best thing that could have ever happened to me. It just took a paradigm shift for me to see and understand that. If it wasn't for this manager, I would still be working at the same station, complacent, wondering if there was more for me…wondering if I would ever find my true purpose. We often hear about people "jumping" and taking the first step. Well, sometimes in life, you have to be pushed. I know I did. When you're pushed and you have no other option, you will always find a way to connect the dots and win. You will always find your way, if you have the will and drive to succeed.

In life, you have to get to a point where you are uncomfortable being comfortable. That's where growth comes from. You have to get comfortable being uncomfortable and vice versa. If you're comfortable, that means it's time for a change. Comfort means conformity…it is time to do the thing that scares you, so that you can win. That is how it works. Never let someone's opinion of you become your reality. *Make* your reality. It's all at your fingertips. I thank this manager for what he did, because it made me a stronger and better person for it. It was exactly the push that I needed (even though it didn't feel like it at the time). I needed to be uncomfortable. It was through the discomfort that led to so many other great opportunities. We may not always understand why something happens to us, but the truth is revealed later as to exactly why it happened. Don't paddle upstream; turn around and allow yourself to flow downstream. You're still going to get to the same place, but instead of fighting the process, let it happen naturally.

Getting back to the story of my demotion, I was on the air hosting a television show in a major TV market. I signed off: "Thank you for watching, I'll see you back here tomorrow!" I walked to my purse sitting in the corner of the room, grabbed my cell phone, and saw a text that read "Urgent. Meeting upstairs. Now." I thought, "That's strange," and proceeded to head upstairs. While walking toward the stairs, a co-worker said, "Hey, I think some people are looking for you upstairs." I smiled and nodded and proceeded to the stairs. When I walked into the large meeting room, I saw my managers, and my entire team sitting in front of me.

"Have a seat," a manger said. I had walked into a room full of co-workers; my entire production team, most of whom also had no idea what was going on, "The show you just finished was your last show. You will no longer be on air in that capacity." He said. The whole room gasped. I kept a poker face, but on the inside, I was thinking, *What just happened? Did I do something wrong? What the heck?* The manager asked, "Do you have any questions?" I sat in silence; my mouth literally was locked shut. It took about 20 seconds to speak, which felt like a lifetime.

I finally was able to murmur out, "May I please speak with you in private?" I was mortified, humiliated, confused, and so hurt. I went into an office and asked the million-dollar question, "Do I still have a job?"

"Yes," the manager said.

I said, "What am I going to do?"

The manager asked, "What would you *like* to do?" I was so confused. *Is this a trick question?* I thought to myself. Then the manager said, "Your option is to be a reporter, or you can walk out those doors and never come back. It's up to you." That was it. I thanked him for his time. Using every ounce of my strength to pull it together, I walked to the parking lot and got into my car.

I took out my cell phone and called my husband. I was bawling profusely. I cried so loudly, I couldn't hear him over the tears and the pain. My husband said, "Just come home. It is all going to work out. Trust me." I went home and my rock, my husband, said, "Tomorrow, you're going back into the office. You're going to walk in with full confidence, looking like a million bucks, and own your new role. That is what you are going to do." He was right. I had a choice…break down and cry or keep my power and rise to the occasion.

The next day when I walked in the office, I was greeted by so many somber faces saying and asking me, "Are you okay?" "I heard what happened." "That's B.S." "What are you going to do?" "Aww, I'm so sorry for you."

To each one, I looked them in the eyes with full confidence and a bright smile and said, "I'm excellent. I have never been better." You see, I had my health, my faith, my family, my tribe, my skillsets, my aspirations… I was so blessed in so many ways, and I chose to focus on the good. I focused on what I *did* have. The morning editorial meeting started, and a manger looked around the room and said, "Who wants to pitch stories first?"

I was the first to raise my hand. "I do," I said. That morning, something energetically was working through me. Not only did I enterprise the lead story for the day, but it was focused on heroin overdoses. I was able to inspire a current addict—who was gearing up to seek help—to go on camera with me and share his story. He even agreed to show his face on camera.

When the day came to a close, many coworkers approached me saying, "Wow, I cannot believe you!" "You inspire me." "I can't believe this happened to you yesterday and not only did you show up, you look amazing, you look more confident than ever and you are producing amazing content."

My response, "It's my job and my integrity." You see, life is not what happens to you. It's what you decide to do with it.

I had a choice. I chose to not let anyone's decisions about me affect ME and my work. I remained a reporter in this position for six months. It was a hard transition, because I had always been an anchor, but I kept the vision of anchoring in front of me at all times and never lost sight of that aspiration. I'll never forget the day I was in the television live truck with a photographer and we were on our way to a story.

He said, "You're a reporter."

I was quick to correct him, saying, "I am an anchor."

He argued, "No, you're a reporter."

I corrected him again and said, "I am an anchor who happens to be reporting." Do you see the difference?

I never owned that present reality because that was not my reality. I held that constant vision of what I was going to achieve in life, and that's what kept me moving forward. Figure out what it is that you want, and don't let anyone sway you. Les

Brown said, "Someone's opinion of you does not have to become your reality." I went on to land the main anchor position at the number one station in Kansas City just six months later...hold on the *vision*. It will all pay off.

I kept working hard and performing above average every single day. Eventually, I met with my boss and told him I wanted to do some long-form investigative stories. He agreed and liked the idea. I did an in-depth story on sex trafficking in northeast Ohio, I covered an in-depth report about African Americans drowning at alarming rates, and went on to cover the Republican National Convention when it rolled though Cleveland. After my coverage of the RNC, my boss pulled me into his office after and said, "Where did *that* come from? Wow..."

I said, "It's been there all along—you just didn't see it." The next day, I was back in the field doing more coverage, and when I returned to the station, my boss reiterated his point from the day prior. He wanted to see if we could talk again about my position. He wanted to keep me in the role of a reporter, to which I again graciously declined. "I am an anchor," I told him, "I am just reporting right now to build my experience and credibility." Then with a warm smile, I looked at him and said, "I remember a few months ago when you said I could walk out the door and never come back."

I will never forget his response to me, and this is a direct quote, "That's because I didn't realize what I had."

This is not a story to rub anything in anyone's face. This is a story of inspiration to empower you to keep pushing forward, even when it feels like the world is crumbling underneath you. Keep pushing, keep striving, keep your vision of what you want in front of you. Two years after that incident, I reached out to my former boss and said, "Thank you." Yes, I said thank you, because if it wasn't for him pushing me, I wouldn't be where I am today. He gave me one of my greatest gifts in this journey we call life. I wouldn't have pushed 1,000 times harder, and I would not have won my first Emmy. You see, it was my live news coverage of the Republican National Convention that won me my very first Emmy. The same year, I also received an Emmy nomination for Best News Anchor. And I went on to be hired as the main evening anchor at the number one station in Kansas City.

Gratitude is not always easy to show, especially to those who do the worst things imaginable to us—even *if* they set us up for great opportunities later on! But one thing I can honestly say about gratitude is that it is a ***magnet*** for bigger and better opportunities. I can't perfectly articulate it, but somehow when we are thankful—even for the things that sting us—better always finds us. Don't give up where you are. Don't stop. Gratitude where you are might not be easy, but think about all the amazing opportunities you can make yourself available for. Think about how much further along you will be when you thank people for the stones they throw at you and use them to build your empire! I have made some of the hardest "thank-you's" in my life. But now, it's ***your*** turn. After the prompt, write the first three things that come to mind:

Gratitude

Now, I want to gently remind you that as you formulate your definition about gratitude means to you, that your definition works for or with the three things that you have written above. Therefore, below define what gratitude means to you:

_____

_____

_____

Excellent! You've completed all four of your definitions! This means that you now have what you need in order to reach for your aspirations in the best way that you possibly can! Now, we can put a bookmark in this page and delve into self-care in the next section.

SELF-CARE
The Power of Your Thoughts

"Every thought plants a seed in your mind…over time, those seeds will grow and affect your mind."

– Unknown

Yes, I Can

Self-care can look like a lot of different things. Sometimes, self-care can be a statement you tell yourself over and over again until you accomplish something. I will share with you another story of my life where I demonstrated one of the best self-care decisions I could have ever made. But let me be the first to tell you: it was not easy.

I have had a lot of high highs and a lot of low lows in my life, many of which would shock most people. I almost failed out of college. Most people don't know that. My freshman year, I was so happy to be independent that I chose parties over purpose. I'll never forget the day I failed statistics. Yep, literally failed the entire course. It was the same day I met with a counselor who gave me one of the greatest wake-up calls of my life. She told me, "You're not going to make it into the J-School (journalism school). Your GPA is just too low." Now, let me tell you something about me: I was *born* to be a journalist; I had been hosting TV shows since the age of 14, so in my mind, I was destined to do this—there was no other option. That was my aspiration, and that was the only future I knew. It was in that moment that I woke up.

I put my big girl pants on and with sheer confidence, even though I was trembling on the inside, asked, "How can I make this right?"

"You can't," she said.

"Yes, I can. I am willing to make this right, just please tell me what I need to do."

She got out her calculator and began punching numbers. She looked down and was silent then looked up at me. "The only way you will make it into the J-School is to get a 4.0 every semester for the next 3 semesters. Dhomonique, you may want to start looking at other options." I swallowed hard. I knew if I wanted something badly enough in life—and I did—I would *have* to put in the work and make my dream a reality.

I made a clean slate of my life. I inventoried my circle and started the process of eliminating people who were draining my energy, spirit, and purpose; those who subconsciously wanted to see me down, rather than up. I studied day and night. I never went out once past 7:00 p.m. during those three semesters, and I earned my 4.0 every single time. I made it into the J-School by just a pinch, and went on to lead a very successful television career earning three Emmy Awards and numerous nominations for my journalistic excellence. Life throws things at you all the time, and you have a choice—*remember that*—you **always** have a choice of how you respond to things. I chose to see this situation as an opportunity and a second chance and, therefore, I rose to the occasion.

I hope this story inspires you to take care of your environment and your atmosphere. To let nothing get in the way of stopping you from achieving your goals and aspirations, even if that means getting yourself out of your own way.

The Injustice on Self-Care

Yes, I do believe we actually do self-care an injustice. Why? Because self-care has an aspect to it that we often don't give enough attention. We talk about disconnecting from routines. We talk about doing something just for ourselves. We talk about respecting our time and space. However, we often forget about the most important facet of self-care: our thoughts.

What good is it if we recite our daily affirmations and aspirations while worrying about everything we have to get done today? How effective are we when we go on social media breaks and spend our idle time beating ourselves up? We literally cancel out all of the positive effects of our self-care methods when we don't first tame our thoughts. Our thoughts are powerful—some are more critical than others. For example, there was a thought you believed this morning or earlier today that may have set the entire tone for the outcome of your day. In another example, going back to before you were born, there was a thought your parents shared and acted upon the day you were conceived. Both of those thoughts were powerful, in that they both determined the production of evident, tangible outcomes in your life. However, one of those thoughts was more crucial than the other—otherwise you might not even be here today!

To ignore the weight of our thoughts—especially our negative thoughts—in terms of our self-care will have serious ramifications. Self-care is like exercise: in order for you to really see the positive benefits, you have to do it routinely, repetitively, and consistently. Controlling your thoughts is like bathing: as long as you maintain it regularly, you will be fine, but when you forget to maintain it, those around you *will* notice. As long as you tame your thoughts regularly, your sense of normalcy will become more stable. Your emotions, mentalities, reactions, dispositions, perspectives, and even your assumptions will begin to balance as you continue to tame your thoughts.

The Infection of Projection

Projection, according to Merianne Corey, is defined as "disowning certain aspects of ourselves by assigning them to our environment. It is when the attributes of our personality that are inconsistent with our self-image are disowned and put onto... other people; hence we blame others for a lot of our problems (Corey, 2014)." Corey goes on to say, "By seeing in others the very qualities that we refuse to acknowledge in ourselves, we avoid taking responsibility for our own feelings and the person who we are, and this keeps us powerless to initiate change (Corey, 2014)."

Although it is true that there may have been a point in time that we have done this to other people, there are times when others project their own problems and shortcomings on to us. Projection, at its source, is a fear or a discomfort with personal responsibility. Sometimes, when the people around you do not give themselves permission to change, they become very uncomfortable and unstable when you are doing something to change yourself. We may not ever admit it to ourselves, but *we* are as much a part of their ecology as their jobs or families are.

Anytime an aspect of someone's ecology changes, it is natural that one feels instable and uncomfortable, but sometimes, they express this discomfort as unwarranted projection on to us when we try to better ourselves.

So, it is only natural that when *we* change, the system of those we are connected to also changes. For some people, they are able to adapt to our growth. But when someone we are connected to is not able to adapt to our growth right away, they may project onto us a struggle that they are dealing with. Someone's opinion of you does not have to be *your* reality. Understand that others' negativity is a reflection on the other person, not you. Never allow the projection of others to infect your aspirations. If there is anything that you want to protect with a vengeance, protect your aspirations by any means necessary.

Do You – Give and Take

I believe that everyone is naturally a giver. In some way, even if you were not aware of it, you are actually giving all the time. Whether it's work, parenting, school, or even community work, you are always giving in some way, shape, or form. This may manifest in you giving your time, your energy, your money, or even your resources or connections. Whatever your philosophy is on being a giver, I'm sure that we can all agree that giving is like pouring out of a pitcher. As beautiful as your generosity is, it has a limitation.

Your generosity and ability to give is limited by how much you are able to *receive* and also by how much you *currently have*. Sometimes, we are able to give beyond our means, but not all of the time. At some point, we will notice the tolling effect that giving has. Now, don't get me wrong, generosity does have its benefits. Little random acts of kindness are in and of themselves a gift to the giver. However, it is healthy to have a system in place that balances how much we give. This is why it is okay to receive.

If the Niagara Falls were to suddenly stop receiving water from its source, it would no longer be able to produce its tremendous beauty. The only reason the Niagara Falls is able to give out so much water is because it receives much water. Every waterfall has a receiving source; once the source goes dry, or is blocked, the waterfall stops. Likewise, if you plug up or block your source or it goes dry, your ability to give will be diminished. Therefore, it is not only okay to receive sometimes, but it is necessary. Make sure that you have a "source"—that someone can replenish your "pitcher." As much as you aspire to *give*, ensure that this is the level that you are able to **receive**.

It does sound like a nice sentiment, but sometimes, this is actually much easier said than done. Sometimes, it is difficult for some to be able to receive, not because they don't know how to say thank you or they don't know how to ask for help, but because they don't know how to be *vulnerable*. The etymology of "vulnerable" suggests that the root meaning of the word is "to be in a position to be wounded". On one hand, it's one thing for me to ask help from you because I have no other option—if you say no, I can reason that it's because you don't have, not because you don't like me. However, it's another thing for me to ask if we can just hang out—if you say no, I might believe it's because you don't like me. To put myself in the line of fire for that kind of rejection is often more painful than asking for help, primarily because I did not *have* to ask you. Sometimes, necessity helps us to make peace with our vulnerability, so that we don't feel like we are being wounded by someone telling us "no" that they are unable to help us.

Make Your Soul Shine

What do I mean when I say, "Make your soul shine"? It can mean more than one thing. I think it means to be who you truly are, even at the disapproval of others. I think it means to be true to yourself and not get drowned out by the opinions of others. Regardless of how I define this, one thing I can definitely say is that shining can sometimes be a very hard thing to do.

What is that one thing you would do for free? What is that thing you do that you wake up thinking about and go to bed thinking about? What is that one thing that makes you smile whenever you think about doing it? That is what makes your soul shine. That is the thing that makes your soul shine. When you do that, whatever it is—writing, dancing, nursing, or planning—you literally become the most authentic version of yourself. When you are the most authentic version of yourself, it is easier for opportunities to find you.

Think of it this way: when you do things that don't make your soul shine all the time, you become a false version of yourself—it's kind of like you are wearing a disguise or a mask, just for the sake of fitting in where you are. But when you are the truest version of yourself—truly authentic—that mask comes off, and you become more recognizable. Yes, this may mean that some people may reject you for being fully authentic, but if the people around you only accept the false version of you—are they the people you want to be around? In the end, it's up to you. But if you really want to make your soul shine, you **have** to be true to yourself.

HOLISTIC BEING
Health, Wealth, Spirituality & Gratitude

"Get health. No labor, effort, nor exercise that can gain it must be grudged." – Ralph Waldo Emerson

"Wealth isn't how much money you have; it's how many people you know." – Chris Rock

"I remember when my mother died. I was so grieved, I stopped talking. I didn't speak for weeks. People sent me cards, flowers, and everything to cheer me up, but it didn't work. When I returned to church, there was a guest preacher preaching in my stead. The topic of his sermon wasn't even on grief; it was about the Holy Spirit. …Eventually, he prompted the congregation to speak in tongues, and I opened up my mouth and began to pray in the Holy Spirit. Suddenly, all the grief that had been pent up inside me released and lifted like a weight off my chest. That day, I learned that emotions exist apart from spirituality. No wonder all of the emotional affirmations of comfort didn't work; it was because my grief was not emotional. My mother's death grieved me in my spirit."
– Bishop T. D. Jakes

"Learn to enjoy every minute of your life. Be happy now. Don't wait for something outside of yourself to

make you happy in the future." – Earl Nightingale
"When you are grateful for what you have, you will
have more." – Oprah Winfrey

Four Dimensions of Being

Earlier in the text, we touched on the topic of the four aspects of a self-made life: health, wealth, spirit, and gratitude. These four aspects are also what I like to call the four dimensions of being, which is how we achieve a sense of wholeness within ourselves that enables us to maintain our aspirations more easily. We took the time to define each one for ourselves, making our aspirations more attainable for us. Now, let's apply our definitions of these four dimensions. This will help us to establish our holistic being, completing our process of resetting ourselves. Let's briefly review our definitions, first. However, because you defined your own definitions, I want you to write them down below (it's okay to look back if you have to)!

For me, health is: _____

_____

For me, wealth is: _____

_____

For me, spirituality is: _____

_____

For me, gratitude is: _____

_____

All for One and One for All

Health, wealth, spirituality, and gratitude: they all work together interchangeably. You may progress in one and regress in another in the same day. To recap, a **progression** is when you handle or respond to a situation with better skills, decisions, and/ or a better attitude than you might have otherwise responded in previous times. A **regression** is when you revert back to a more primitive mental and/or emotional way after you have made a progression in that same part of yourself. I am by no means telling you that you must progress in all four aspects all of the time. That's unrealistic. What you *can* do is to recognize when you are progressing and when you are regressing. It's the awareness of where you are in your journey that allows you to handle the curves of life a little better.

And what is so beautiful about these four aspects is that when you work on one area, often, it helps you progress in all the others! So, you don't have to scatter your focus when it comes to resetting yourself. You can be present and focus on the current priority—whether that is health, wealth, spirituality, or gratitude. And when you begin to progress in that area of your life, you learn about yourself regarding the other categories, how to better manage or handle them.

> *"The shoe that fits one person pinches another."*
> *– Carl Jung*

Now, let's talk about *you*. When talking about identity in "Self-Defined", we asked ourselves, "Who am I…*really*?" Maybe you still don't have a full answer to that. That's okay. I am going to give you descriptions of **four main groups of people.** Based on research by Dr. Dario Nardi, PhD, who has done research on the neuroscience of personality, there are four main ways people think about and solve similar problems (Nardi, 2011). Based on which group(s) you identify with (you may identify with more than one), you will have a better understanding…not only of who you are, but also of how you can approach your "reset". No two people are the same. I cannot expect a method that worked for me to apply to someone else the exact same way. I want you to take these skills and tools and make it all your own. Use them to *your* total advantage! These next four sections will give you some tips on how to use the journal guide in Part 2 of this book!

If you…

- Are easily overwhelmed
- Are typically foresighted
- Are analytical and creative

You are a *visionary*! You don't need much to get inspired, but you may have a hard time with rigid routines. You need a tight-knit circle of **trusted** loved ones and supporters who can hold you accountable, challenge you, and encourage you (Nardi, 2011).

If you…

- Prefer the bigger picture
- Love nature
- Prefer concrete and applicable information

You are a *ground-runner*! You love your freedom, and you don't like being put in a box. Give yourself one thing to focus on each week and find people who can help you with the smaller details (Nardi, 2011).

If you…

- Are in it for the long haul
- Love the details
- Love organization and clarity

You are a *ruler*! Like a ruler is good for structure and measurement, you provide balance and produce calculated results wherever you go, even if you have to be a perfectionist. Take care of yourself first, and work with people who can step back and see the bigger construct of things (Nardi, 2011).

If y`ou…

- Love to multitask
- Are innovative and unique

- Perform high levels in multiple fields

You are a *juggler*! The abstract doesn't bother you one bit, and you are known for your originality, although you may have a hard time finishing every project you start. Partner with someone who can challenge you when you are only thinking one way and think of ways to liven your duller tasks (Nardi, 2011).

You may be one or more of the above, but regardless of what kind of problem-solver you are, never forget your definitions and use them to guide you back to your center whenever you stray away. Also recognize that sometimes your definitions may change, and that is okay. Those new definitions—in time—will become your new compass to your next level!

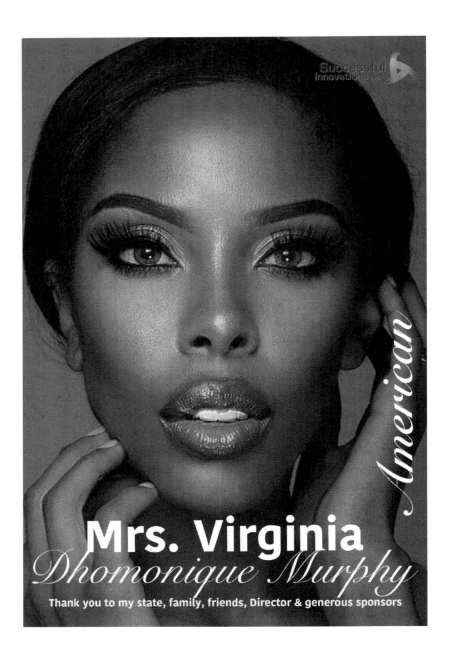

Mrs. Virginia
Dhomonique Murphy

Thank you to my state, family, friends, Director & generous sponsors

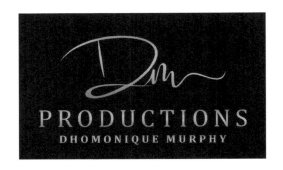

Part 2

LIVING YOUR BEST LIFE

HOW TO USE THIS SYSTEM

Below is an easy-to-follow breakdown of the 30-Day Guided Self-Reset System, which begins on the next page. This journal is so unique, because it is designed to help you help yourself! Each point below will correspond with the parts of the journal, in order:

1. At the top of every journal entry, there is a motivational quote to get you started.

2. There are 30 journal entries for 30 days, however, there is a "date" line beneath each day. This means you may not complete this part of the book in 30 days, and that is okay.

3. The box below the date is for two things:

   a. Your #AOTD (Aspiration of The Day). Aspirations don't change the way goals do, so you may likely be writing the same thing for 30 days. Write down your aspiration every day. This contributes to breaking away the old mindset and is a fundamental part of the resetting process. Remember "A.I.E."...

   b. "And today I will:" This part is for your daily goal. This will change almost every day.

4. Task of the Day: In this box, write down one thing you want to do to reach your goal and aspiration. No matter how big or small, write it down.

5. At the bottom of the first half of every journal entry, there is a more encouraging quote to start you on your way.

6. Whereas steps 1-5 are for your routine first thing in the morning, steps 6-8 are designed for the evening, at the end of your day. For the **reflection**, write in each section something you observed for that day after the prompt. As you fill up your journal, you will see more of the ups and downs, and you may be able to recognize patterns over a period of time. It's important to track yourself so that you can reset yourself.

7. Meditate: You accomplish something every day, and you learn something every day. Use this time to think about and record what you have accomplished and what you learned. This is crucial to the resetting process because this is going to be a major marker for your long-term progress. Being able to look back on past wins and lessons can be really helpful in the future, as well.

8. Reset: Based on how you handled your day, and based on your entries in steps 1-7, score yourself.

   a. **However**: Don't look at the "regression" as "wrong" and the "progression" as "right". Rather, see them as "out" and "in", respectively. Regression just means you're moving further away from your reset, but you can always go back and progress back toward your reset.

   b. The purpose of this part of the journal is just to help you identify when you are getting closer to your reset and when you are moving further away.

   c. Finally, you can reset yourself as many times as you want! Consider yourself "reset" when you complete the 30 journal entries!

30-DAY GUIDED
SELF-RESET SYSTEM

The secret of getting ahead is getting started.
– Mark Twain

DAY 1

DATE: _____

DAILY AFFIRMATION: I ASPIRE TO

_____

_____

_____

AND TODAY, I WILL _____

_____

_____

TASK OF THE DAY

"We can let circumstances rule us, or we can take charge and rule our lives from within."
– Earl Nightingale

REFLECTION

TODAY, MY HEALTH LOOKED LIKE _____

_____

_____

_____

TODAY, MY WEALTH LOOKED LIKE _____

_____

_____

_____

TODAY, MY SPIRITUALITY LOOKED LIKE_____

_____

_____

_____

TODAY, MY GRATITUDE LOOKED LIKE_____

_____

_____

_____

MEDITATE

TODAY, I ACHIEVED _____

_____

_____

_____

AND I LEARNED _____

_____

_____

_____

RESET

OVERALL, TODAY, MY MENTAL "RESET" SCORE WAS:

◯ ◯ ◯ ◯ ◯

1   2   3   4   5

REGRESSION   *PROGRESSION*

*"Nothing can be done without hope and confidence." – **Helen Keller**

DAY 2

DATE: _____

DAILY AFFIRMATION: I ASPIRE TO

_____

_____

_____

AND TODAY, I WILL _____

_____

_____

TASK OF THE DAY

"Everything will be okay in the end. If it's not okay, then it's not the end. " – **Ed Sheeran**

REFLECTION

TODAY, MY HEALTH LOOKED LIKE _____

_____

_____

_____

TODAY, MY WEALTH LOOKED LIKE _____

_____

_____

_____

TODAY, MY SPIRITUALITY LOOKED LIKE_____

_____

_____

_____

TODAY, MY GRATITUDE LOOKED LIKE_____

_____

_____

_____

MEDITATE

TODAY, I ACHIEVED _____

_____

_____

_____

AND I LEARNED _____

_____

_____

_____

RESET

OVERALL, TODAY, MY MENTAL "RESET" SCORE WAS:

| 1 | 2 | 3 | 4 | 5 |

REGRESSION   *PROGRESSION*

*"Look up at the stars and not down at your feet." – **Stephen Hawking***

DAY 3

DATE: _____

┌───┐
│ *DAILY AFFIRMATION: I ASPIRE TO* │
└───┘

_____

_____

_____

AND TODAY, I WILL _____

_____

_____

┌───┐
│   **TASK OF THE DAY**   │
│   │
│   │
│   │
│   │
│   │
│   │
└───┘

"The harder you fall, the heavier your heart; the heavier your heart, the stronger you climb; the stronger you climb, the higher your pedestal. "
– Criss Jami

REFLECTION

TODAY, MY HEALTH LOOKED LIKE _____

_____

_____

_____

TODAY, MY WEALTH LOOKED LIKE _____

_____

_____

_____

TODAY, MY SPIRITUALITY LOOKED LIKE_____

_____

_____

_____

TODAY, MY GRATITUDE LOOKED LIKE_____

_____

_____

_____

MEDITATE

TODAY, I ACHIEVED _____

_____

_____

_____

AND I LEARNED _____

_____

_____

_____

RESET

OVERALL, TODAY, MY MENTAL "RESET" SCORE WAS:

◯ ◯ ◯ ◯ ◯

1   2   3   4   5

REGRESSION   *PROGRESSION*

"If you're going through hell, keep going."
– Winston Churchill

DAY 4

DATE: _____

DAILY AFFIRMATION: I ASPIRE TO

_____

_____

_____

AND TODAY, I WILL _____

_____

_____

TASK OF THE DAY

"Encourage yourself, believe in yourself, and love yourself. Never doubt who you are. "
– Stephanie Lahart

REFLECTION

TODAY, MY HEALTH LOOKED LIKE _____

_____

_____

_____

TODAY, MY WEALTH LOOKED LIKE _____

_____

_____

_____

TODAY, MY SPIRITUALITY LOOKED LIKE_____

_____

_____

_____

TODAY, MY GRATITUDE LOOKED LIKE_____

_____

_____

_____

MEDITATE

TODAY, I ACHIEVED _____

_____

_____

_____

AND I LEARNED _____

_____

_____

_____

RESET

OVERALL, TODAY, MY MENTAL "RESET" SCORE WAS:

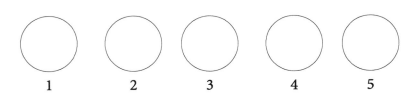

| 1 | 2 | 3 | 4 | 5 |

REGRESSION   *PROGRESSION*

"Do the difficult things while they are easy, and do the great things while they are small."
– Lao Tzu

DAY 5

DATE: _____

DAILY AFFIRMATION: I ASPIRE TO

_____

_____

_____

AND TODAY, I WILL _____

_____

TASK OF THE DAY

"The greatest act of faith some days is to simply get up and face another day. " – Amy Gatliff

REFLECTION

TODAY, MY HEALTH LOOKED LIKE _____

_____

_____

_____

TODAY, MY WEALTH LOOKED LIKE _____

_____

_____

_____

TODAY, MY SPIRITUALITY LOOKED LIKE_____

_____

_____

_____

TODAY, MY GRATITUDE LOOKED LIKE_____

_____

_____

_____

MEDITATE

TODAY, I ACHIEVED _____

_____

_____

_____

AND I LEARNED _____

_____

_____

_____

RESET

OVERALL, TODAY, MY MENTAL "RESET" SCORE WAS:

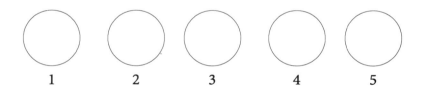

1   2   3   4   5

REGRESSION   *PROGRESSION*

"Quality is not an act; it is a habit."
– Aristotle

DAY 6

DATE: _____

DAILY AFFIRMATION: I ASPIRE TO

_____

_____

_____

AND TODAY, I WILL _____

_____

_____

TASK OF THE DAY

"Everything is within your power, and your power is within you. " – **Janice Trachtman**

REFLECTION

TODAY, MY HEALTH LOOKED LIKE _____

_____

_____

_____

TODAY, MY WEALTH LOOKED LIKE _____

_____

_____

_____

TODAY, MY SPIRITUALITY LOOKED LIKE_____

_____

_____

_____

TODAY, MY GRATITUDE LOOKED LIKE_____

_____

_____

_____

MEDITATE

TODAY, I ACHIEVED _____

_____

_____

_____

AND I LEARNED _____

_____

_____

_____

RESET

OVERALL, TODAY, MY MENTAL "RESET" SCORE WAS:

◯ ◯ ◯ ◯ ◯

1   2   3   4   5

REGRESSION   *PROGRESSION*

"Knowing is not enough; we must apply.
Willing is not enough; we must do."
*– **Johann Wolfgang von Goethe***

DAY 7

DATE: _____

DAILY AFFIRMATION: I ASPIRE TO

_____
_____
_____

AND TODAY, I WILL _____

_____

TASK OF THE DAY

*"Renewal requires opening yourself up to new
ways of thinking and feeling. " – **Deborah Day***

REFLECTION

TODAY, MY HEALTH LOOKED LIKE _____

_____

_____

_____

TODAY, MY WEALTH LOOKED LIKE _____

_____

_____

_____

TODAY, MY SPIRITUALITY LOOKED LIKE_____

_____

_____

_____

TODAY, MY GRATITUDE LOOKED LIKE_____

_____

_____

_____

MEDITATE

TODAY, I ACHIEVED _____

_____

_____

_____

AND I LEARNED _____

_____

_____

_____

RESET

OVERALL, TODAY, MY MENTAL "RESET" SCORE WAS:

   1   2   3   4   5

REGRESSION   *PROGRESSION*

"Accept the challenges so that you can feel the exhilaration of victory." – **George S. Patton**

DAY 8

DATE: _____

DAILY AFFIRMATION: I ASPIRE TO

_____

_____

_____

AND TODAY, I WILL _____

_____

_____

TASK OF THE DAY

"It is not the mountain we conquer, but ourselves. "
– Edmund Hillary

REFLECTION

TODAY, MY HEALTH LOOKED LIKE _____

_____

_____

_____

TODAY, MY WEALTH LOOKED LIKE _____

_____

_____

_____

TODAY, MY SPIRITUALITY LOOKED LIKE_____

_____

_____

_____

TODAY, MY GRATITUDE LOOKED LIKE_____

_____

_____

_____

MEDITATE

TODAY, I ACHIEVED _____

_____

_____

_____

AND I LEARNED _____

_____

_____

_____

RESET

OVERALL, TODAY, MY MENTAL "RESET" SCORE WAS:

◯	◯	◯	◯	◯
1	2	3	4	5

REGRESSION   *PROGRESSION*

"It always seems impossible until it's done."
– Nelson Mandela

DAY 9

DATE: _____

DAILY AFFIRMATION: I ASPIRE TO

_____

_____

_____

AND TODAY, I WILL _____

_____

_____

TASK OF THE DAY

"Experience is a brutal teacher, but you learn.
My God, do you learn. " – **C. S. Lewis**

REFLECTION

TODAY, MY HEALTH LOOKED LIKE _____

_____

_____

_____

TODAY, MY WEALTH LOOKED LIKE _____

_____

_____

_____

TODAY, MY SPIRITUALITY LOOKED LIKE_____

_____

_____

_____

TODAY, MY GRATITUDE LOOKED LIKE_____

_____

_____

_____

MEDITATE

TODAY, I ACHIEVED _____

_____

_____

_____

AND I LEARNED _____

_____

_____

_____

RESET

OVERALL, TODAY, MY MENTAL "RESET" SCORE WAS:

◯ ◯ ◯ ◯ ◯

1   2   3   4   5

REGRESSION   *PROGRESSION*

*"When you reach the end of your rope, tie a knot in it and hang on." – **Franklin D. Roosevelt***

DAY 10

DATE: _____

DAILY AFFIRMATION: I ASPIRE TO

_____

_____

_____

AND TODAY, I WILL _____

_____

_____

TASK OF THE DAY

"Don't wait. The time will never be just right. *" – Napoleon Hill*

REFLECTION

TODAY, MY HEALTH LOOKED LIKE _____

_____

_____

_____

TODAY, MY WEALTH LOOKED LIKE _____

_____

_____

_____

TODAY, MY SPIRITUALITY LOOKED LIKE_____

_____

_____

_____

TODAY, MY GRATITUDE LOOKED LIKE_____

_____

_____

_____

MEDITATE

TODAY, I ACHIEVED _____

_____

_____

_____

AND I LEARNED _____

_____

_____

_____

RESET

OVERALL, TODAY, MY MENTAL "RESET" SCORE WAS:

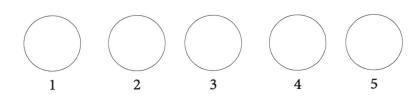

   1   2   3   4   5

REGRESSION   *PROGRESSION*

"You can't build a reputation on what you are going to do."
– Henry Ford

DAY 11

DATE: _____

DAILY AFFIRMATION: I ASPIRE TO

_____

_____

_____

AND TODAY, I WILL _____

_____

_____

TASK OF THE DAY

"Motivation comes from working on things we care about. " – **Sheryl Sandberg**

REFLECTION

TODAY, MY HEALTH LOOKED LIKE _____

_____

_____

_____

TODAY, MY WEALTH LOOKED LIKE _____

_____

_____

_____

TODAY, MY SPIRITUALITY LOOKED LIKE_____

_____

_____

_____

TODAY, MY GRATITUDE LOOKED LIKE_____

_____

_____

_____

MEDITATE

TODAY, I ACHIEVED _____

_____

_____

_____

AND I LEARNED _____

_____

_____

_____

RESET

OVERALL, TODAY, MY MENTAL "RESET" SCORE WAS:

◯   ◯   ◯   ◯   ◯

1   2   3   4   5

REGRESSION   *PROGRESSION*

*"Life is 10 percent what happens to you and 90 percent how you react to it." – **Charles R. Swindoll***

DAY 12

DATE: _____

> *DAILY AFFIRMATION: I ASPIRE TO*

_____
_____
_____

AND TODAY, I WILL _____
_____
_____

TASK OF THE DAY

"You don't need to see the whole staircase, just take the first step. " – **Martin Luther King, Jr.**

REFLECTION

TODAY, MY HEALTH LOOKED LIKE _____

_____

_____

_____

TODAY, MY WEALTH LOOKED LIKE _____

_____

_____

_____

TODAY, MY SPIRITUALITY LOOKED LIKE_____

_____

_____

_____

TODAY, MY GRATITUDE LOOKED LIKE_____

_____

_____

_____

MEDITATE

TODAY, I ACHIEVED _____

_____

_____

_____

AND I LEARNED _____

_____

_____

_____

RESET

OVERALL, TODAY, MY MENTAL "RESET" SCORE WAS:

◯　　◯　　◯　　◯　　◯

1　　　2　　　3　　　4　　　5

REGRESSION　　　　　　　*PROGRESSION*

"Well done is better than well said."
– Benjamin Franklin

DAY 13

DATE: _____

┌─────────────────────────────────────┐
│ *DAILY AFFIRMATION: I ASPIRE TO* │
└─────────────────────────────────────┘

_____

_____

_____

AND TODAY, I WILL _____

_____

_____

┌─────────────────────────────────────┐
│ **TASK OF THE DAY** │
│ │
│ │
│ │
│ │
│ │
│ │
│ │
└─────────────────────────────────────┘

*"I am not a product of my circumstances. I am a product of my decisions." – **Stephen Covey***

REFLECTION

TODAY, MY HEALTH LOOKED LIKE _____

_____

_____

_____

TODAY, MY WEALTH LOOKED LIKE _____

_____

_____

_____

TODAY, MY SPIRITUALITY LOOKED LIKE_____

_____

_____

_____

TODAY, MY GRATITUDE LOOKED LIKE_____

_____

_____

_____

MEDITATE

TODAY, I ACHIEVED _____

_____

_____

_____

AND I LEARNED _____

_____

_____

_____

RESET

OVERALL, TODAY, MY MENTAL "RESET" SCORE WAS:

◯ ◯ ◯ ◯ ◯

1   2   3   4   5

REGRESSION   *PROGRESSION*

"If you can dream it, you can do it." – **Walt Disney**

DAY 14

DATE: _____

DAILY AFFIRMATION: I ASPIRE TO

_____

_____

_____

AND TODAY, I WILL _____

_____

_____

TASK OF THE DAY

"When life gives you a hundred reasons to break down and cry, show life that you have a million reasons to smile and laugh. Stay strong. **" - Unknown**

REFLECTION

TODAY, MY HEALTH LOOKED LIKE _____

_____

_____

_____

TODAY, MY WEALTH LOOKED LIKE _____

_____

_____

_____

TODAY, MY SPIRITUALITY LOOKED LIKE_____

_____

_____

_____

TODAY, MY GRATITUDE LOOKED LIKE_____

_____

_____

_____

MEDITATE

TODAY, I ACHIEVED _____

_____

_____

_____

AND I LEARNED _____

_____

_____

_____

RESET

OVERALL, TODAY, MY MENTAL "RESET" SCORE WAS:

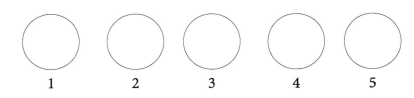

| 1 | 2 | 3 | 4 | 5 |

REGRESSION   *PROGRESSION*

"Things do not happen. Things are made to happen."
*– **John F. Kennedy***

DAY 15

DATE: _____

DAILY AFFIRMATION: I ASPIRE TO

_____

_____

_____

AND TODAY, I WILL _____

_____

_____

TASK OF THE DAY

"Don't worry about failures; worry about the chances you miss when you don't even try. " –
Jack Canfield

REFLECTION

TODAY, MY HEALTH LOOKED LIKE _____

_____

_____

_____

TODAY, MY WEALTH LOOKED LIKE _____

_____

_____

_____

TODAY, MY SPIRITUALITY LOOKED LIKE_____

_____

_____

_____

TODAY, MY GRATITUDE LOOKED LIKE_____

_____

_____

_____

MEDITATE

TODAY, I ACHIEVED _____

_____

_____

_____

AND I LEARNED _____

_____

_____

_____

RESET

OVERALL, TODAY, MY MENTAL "RESET" SCORE WAS:

◯ ◯ ◯ ◯ ◯

1   2   3   4   5

REGRESSION   *PROGRESSION*

"There's a way to do it better – find it."
– Thomas Edison

DAY 16

DATE: _____

DAILY AFFIRMATION: I ASPIRE TO

_____

_____

_____

AND TODAY, I WILL _____

_____

_____

TASK OF THE DAY

*"The best way to not feel hopeless is to get up
and do something. ...Fill the world with hope,
and you will fill yourself with hope. "*
– Barack Obama

REFLECTION

TODAY, MY HEALTH LOOKED LIKE _____

_____

_____

_____

TODAY, MY WEALTH LOOKED LIKE _____

_____

_____

_____

TODAY, MY SPIRITUALITY LOOKED LIKE_____

_____

_____

_____

TODAY, MY GRATITUDE LOOKED LIKE_____

_____

_____

_____

MEDITATE

TODAY, I ACHIEVED _____

_____

_____

_____

AND I LEARNED _____

_____

_____

_____

RESET

OVERALL, TODAY, MY MENTAL "RESET" SCORE WAS:

◯	◯	◯	◯	◯
1	2	3	4	5

REGRESSION   *PROGRESSION*

*"Sometimes, you need to get knocked down before you can really figure out what your fight is and how you need to fight it." – **Chadwick Boseman***

DAY 17

DATE: _____

> *DAILY AFFIRMATION: I ASPIRE TO*

_____

_____

_____

AND TODAY, I WILL _____

_____

TASK OF THE DAY

"You are enough just as you are. "
– Meghan Markle

REFLECTION

TODAY, MY HEALTH LOOKED LIKE _____

_____

_____

_____

TODAY, MY WEALTH LOOKED LIKE _____

_____

_____

_____

TODAY, MY SPIRITUALITY LOOKED LIKE_____

_____

_____

_____

TODAY, MY GRATITUDE LOOKED LIKE_____

_____

_____

_____

MEDITATE

TODAY, I ACHIEVED _____

_____

_____

_____

AND I LEARNED _____

_____

_____

_____

RESET

OVERALL, TODAY, MY MENTAL "RESET" SCORE WAS:

◯   ◯   ◯   ◯   ◯

1   2   3   4   5

REGRESSION   *PROGRESSION*

"Everything negative—pressure, challenges—is all an opportunity for me to rise." – **Kobe Bryant**

DAY 18

DATE: _____

DAILY AFFIRMATION: I ASPIRE TO

_____

_____

_____

AND TODAY, I WILL _____

_____

_____

TASK OF THE DAY

"Don't be pushed by your problems. Be led by your dreams. " – **Ralph Waldo Emerson**

REFLECTION

TODAY, MY HEALTH LOOKED LIKE _____

_____

_____

_____

TODAY, MY WEALTH LOOKED LIKE _____

_____

_____

_____

TODAY, MY SPIRITUALITY LOOKED LIKE_____

_____

_____

_____

TODAY, MY GRATITUDE LOOKED LIKE_____

_____

_____

_____

MEDITATE

TODAY, I ACHIEVED _____

_____

_____

_____

AND I LEARNED _____

_____

_____

_____

RESET

OVERALL, TODAY, MY MENTAL "RESET" SCORE WAS:

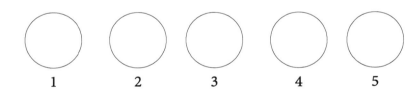

| 1 | 2 | 3 | 4 | 5 |

REGRESSION　　　　　　　　　　*PROGRESSION*

"You've got to have faith in what you're doing and not take no for an answer." – **Nipsey Hussle**

DAY 19

DATE: _____

DAILY AFFIRMATION: I ASPIRE TO

_____

_____

_____

AND TODAY, I WILL _____

_____

_____

TASK OF THE DAY

*"Challenges are what make life interesting, and overcoming them is what makes life meaningful. " – **Joshua Marine**

REFLECTION

TODAY, MY HEALTH LOOKED LIKE _____

_____

_____

_____

TODAY, MY WEALTH LOOKED LIKE _____

_____

_____

_____

TODAY, MY SPIRITUALITY LOOKED LIKE_____

_____

_____

_____

TODAY, MY GRATITUDE LOOKED LIKE_____

_____

_____

_____

MEDITATE

TODAY, I ACHIEVED _____

_____

_____

_____

AND I LEARNED _____

_____

_____

_____

RESET

OVERALL, TODAY, MY MENTAL "RESET" SCORE WAS:

◯   ◯   ◯   ◯   ◯

1   2   3   4   5

REGRESSION   *PROGRESSION*

*"We have this window of opportunity; we have a chance to make something real happen. ...This chance won't come around again." – **Michelle Obama***

DAY 20

DATE: _____

DAILY AFFIRMATION: I ASPIRE TO

_____

_____

_____

AND TODAY, I WILL _____

_____

_____

TASK OF THE DAY

"Don't harp on the negative, because if you do, there's no progression. " – **Taraji P. Henson**

REFLECTION

TODAY, MY HEALTH LOOKED LIKE _____

_____

_____

_____

TODAY, MY WEALTH LOOKED LIKE _____

_____

_____

_____

TODAY, MY SPIRITUALITY LOOKED LIKE_____

_____

_____

_____

TODAY, MY GRATITUDE LOOKED LIKE_____

_____

_____

_____

MEDITATE

TODAY, I ACHIEVED _____

_____

_____

_____

AND I LEARNED _____

_____

_____

_____

RESET

OVERALL, TODAY, MY MENTAL "RESET" SCORE WAS:

◯　　◯　　◯　　◯　　◯

1　　　2　　　3　　　4　　　5

REGRESSION　　　　　　*PROGRESSION*

"Ambition is the path to success. Persistence is the vehicle you arrive in." – **Bill Bradley**

DAY 21

DATE: _____

DAILY AFFIRMATION: I ASPIRE TO

_____

_____

_____

AND TODAY, I WILL _____

_____

_____

TASK OF THE DAY

"You pray for rain, you gotta deal with the mud, too. That's a part of it. " – **Denzel Washington**

REFLECTION

TODAY, MY HEALTH LOOKED LIKE _____

_____

_____

_____

TODAY, MY WEALTH LOOKED LIKE _____

_____

_____

_____

TODAY, MY SPIRITUALITY LOOKED LIKE_____

_____

_____

_____

TODAY, MY GRATITUDE LOOKED LIKE_____

_____

_____

_____

MEDITATE

TODAY, I ACHIEVED _____

_____

_____

_____

AND I LEARNED _____

_____

_____

_____

RESET

OVERALL, TODAY, MY MENTAL "RESET" SCORE WAS:

◯   ◯   ◯   ◯   ◯

1   2   3   4   5

REGRESSION   *PROGRESSION*

"Attitude is a little thing that makes a big difference." –
Winston Churchill

DAY 22

DATE: _____

DAILY AFFIRMATION: I ASPIRE TO

_____

_____

_____

AND TODAY, I WILL _____

_____

_____

TASK OF THE DAY

"I discovered that joy is not the negation of pain, but rather acknowledging the presence of pain and feeling happiness, in spite of it. " –
Lupita Nyong'o

REFLECTION

TODAY, MY HEALTH LOOKED LIKE _____

_____

_____

_____

TODAY, MY WEALTH LOOKED LIKE _____

_____

_____

_____

TODAY, MY SPIRITUALITY LOOKED LIKE_____

_____

_____

_____

TODAY, MY GRATITUDE LOOKED LIKE_____

_____

_____

_____

MEDITATE

TODAY, I ACHIEVED _____

_____

_____

_____

AND I LEARNED _____

_____

_____

_____

RESET

OVERALL, TODAY, MY MENTAL "RESET" SCORE WAS:

◯   ◯   ◯   ◯   ◯

1   2   3   4   5

REGRESSION   *PROGRESSION*

"Excellence is not a skill; it's an attitude."
– Ralph Marston

DAY 23

DATE: _____

DAILY AFFIRMATION: I ASPIRE TO

_____

_____

_____

AND TODAY, I WILL _____

_____

_____

TASK OF THE DAY

"Put blinders onto those things that conspire to hold you back, especially the ones in your own head. " – **Meryl Streep**

REFLECTION

TODAY, MY HEALTH LOOKED LIKE _____

_____

_____

_____

TODAY, MY WEALTH LOOKED LIKE _____

_____

_____

_____

TODAY, MY SPIRITUALITY LOOKED LIKE_____

_____

_____

_____

TODAY, MY GRATITUDE LOOKED LIKE_____

_____

_____

_____

MEDITATE

TODAY, I ACHIEVED _____

_____

_____

_____

AND I LEARNED _____

_____

_____

_____

RESET

OVERALL, TODAY, MY MENTAL "RESET" SCORE WAS:

◯   ◯   ◯   ◯   ◯

1   2   3   4   5

REGRESSION   *PROGRESSION*

"My mission in life is not merely to survive, but to thrive; and to do so with some passion, some compassion, some humor and some style."
– Maya Angelou

DAY 24

DATE: _____

DAILY AFFIRMATION: I ASPIRE TO

_____

_____

_____

AND TODAY, I WILL _____

_____

_____

TASK OF THE DAY

"Resist your fear; fear will never lead you to a positive end. Go for your faith and what you believe. " – **Bishop T. D. Jakes**

REFLECTION

TODAY, MY HEALTH LOOKED LIKE _____

_____

_____

_____

TODAY, MY WEALTH LOOKED LIKE _____

_____

_____

_____

TODAY, MY SPIRITUALITY LOOKED LIKE_____

_____

_____

_____

TODAY, MY GRATITUDE LOOKED LIKE_____

_____

_____

_____

MEDITATE

TODAY, I ACHIEVED _____

_____

_____

_____

AND I LEARNED _____

_____

_____

_____

RESET

OVERALL, TODAY, MY MENTAL "RESET" SCORE WAS:

◯ ◯ ◯ ◯ ◯

1   2   3   4   5

REGRESSION   *PROGRESSION*

*"The measure of who we are is what we do with what we have." – **Vince Lombardi***

DAY 25

DATE: _____

DAILY AFFIRMATION: I ASPIRE TO

_____
_____
_____

AND TODAY, I WILL _____

_____
_____

TASK OF THE DAY

"Sometimes, good things fall apart so that better things can come together. "
-Marilyn Monroe

REFLECTION

TODAY, MY HEALTH LOOKED LIKE _____

_____

_____

_____

TODAY, MY WEALTH LOOKED LIKE _____

_____

_____

_____

TODAY, MY SPIRITUALITY LOOKED LIKE_____

_____

_____

_____

TODAY, MY GRATITUDE LOOKED LIKE_____

_____

_____

_____

MEDITATE

TODAY, I ACHIEVED _____

_____

_____

_____

AND I LEARNED _____

_____

_____

_____

RESET

OVERALL, TODAY, MY MENTAL "RESET" SCORE WAS:

◯   ◯   ◯   ◯   ◯

1   2   3   4   5

REGRESSION   *PROGRESSION*

*"When something is important enough, you do it, even if the odds are not in your favor." – **Elon Musk**

DAY 26

DATE: _____

DAILY AFFIRMATION: I ASPIRE TO

_____

_____

_____

AND TODAY, I WILL _____

_____

_____

TASK OF THE DAY

"If you can do what you do best and be happy, you are further along in life than most people.
*" – **Leonardo DiCaprio***

REFLECTION

TODAY, MY HEALTH LOOKED LIKE _____

_____

_____

_____

TODAY, MY WEALTH LOOKED LIKE _____

_____

_____

_____

TODAY, MY SPIRITUALITY LOOKED LIKE_____

_____

_____

_____

TODAY, MY GRATITUDE LOOKED LIKE_____

_____

_____

_____

MEDITATE

TODAY, I ACHIEVED _____

_____

_____

_____

AND I LEARNED _____

_____

_____

_____

RESET

OVERALL, TODAY, MY MENTAL "RESET" SCORE WAS:

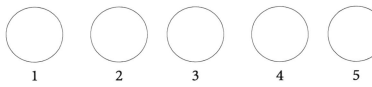

| 1 | 2 | 3 | 4 | 5 |

REGRESSION   *PROGRESSION*

"Failure will never overtake me if my determination to succeed is strong enough." – **Og Mandino**

DAY 27

DATE: _____

> ### *DAILY AFFIRMATION: I ASPIRE TO*

_____

_____

_____

AND TODAY, I WILL _____

_____

_____

> ### **TASK OF THE DAY**

"I say if I'm beautiful. I say if I'm strong. You will not determine my story—I will. "
– Amy Schumer

REFLECTION

TODAY, MY HEALTH LOOKED LIKE _____

_____

_____

_____

TODAY, MY WEALTH LOOKED LIKE _____

_____

_____

_____

TODAY, MY SPIRITUALITY LOOKED LIKE_____

_____

_____

_____

TODAY, MY GRATITUDE LOOKED LIKE_____

_____

_____

_____

MEDITATE

TODAY, I ACHIEVED _____

_____

_____

_____

AND I LEARNED _____

_____

_____

_____

RESET

OVERALL, TODAY, MY MENTAL "RESET" SCORE WAS:

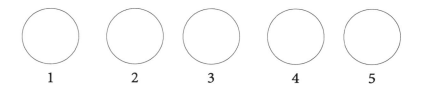

   1   2   3   4   5

REGRESSION   *PROGRESSION*

"If you fell down yesterday, stand up today."
– H. G. Wells

DAY 28

DATE: _____

DAILY AFFIRMATION: I ASPIRE TO

_____

_____

_____

AND TODAY, I WILL _____

_____

_____

TASK OF THE DAY

"There are no regrets in life. Just lessons. "
– Jennifer Aniston

REFLECTION

TODAY, MY HEALTH LOOKED LIKE _____

_____

_____

_____

TODAY, MY WEALTH LOOKED LIKE _____

_____

_____

_____

TODAY, MY SPIRITUALITY LOOKED LIKE_____

_____

_____

_____

TODAY, MY GRATITUDE LOOKED LIKE_____

_____

_____

_____

MEDITATE

TODAY, I ACHIEVED _____

_____

_____

_____

AND I LEARNED _____

_____

_____

_____

RESET

OVERALL, TODAY, MY MENTAL "RESET" SCORE WAS:

◯   ◯   ◯   ◯   ◯

1   2   3   4   5

REGRESSION   *PROGRESSION*

*"Small deeds done are better than great deeds planned." – **Peter Marshall***

DAY 29

DATE: _____

DAILY AFFIRMATION: I ASPIRE TO

_____

_____

_____

AND TODAY, I WILL _____

_____

_____

TASK OF THE DAY

"Perfect is boring. Human is beautiful. " –
Tyra Banks

REFLECTION

TODAY, MY HEALTH LOOKED LIKE _____

_____

_____

_____

TODAY, MY WEALTH LOOKED LIKE _____

_____

_____

_____

TODAY, MY SPIRITUALITY LOOKED LIKE_____

_____

_____

_____

TODAY, MY GRATITUDE LOOKED LIKE_____

_____

_____

_____

MEDITATE

TODAY, I ACHIEVED _____

_____

_____

_____

AND I LEARNED _____

_____

_____

_____

RESET

OVERALL, TODAY, MY MENTAL "RESET" SCORE WAS:

◯   ◯   ◯   ◯   ◯

1   2   3   4   5

REGRESSION   *PROGRESSION*

"Set your goals high, and don't stop until you get there." – **Bo Jackson**

DAY 30

DATE: _____

DAILY AFFIRMATION: I ASPIRE TO

_____

_____

_____

AND TODAY, I WILL _____

_____

_____

TASK OF THE DAY

Be thankful for what you have; you'll end up having more. If you concentrate on what you don't have, you will never, ever have enough.
" – **Oprah Winfrey**

REFLECTION

TODAY, MY HEALTH LOOKED LIKE _____

_____

_____

_____

TODAY, MY WEALTH LOOKED LIKE _____

_____

_____

_____

TODAY, MY SPIRITUALITY LOOKED LIKE_____

_____

_____

_____

TODAY, MY GRATITUDE LOOKED LIKE_____

_____

_____

_____

MEDITATE

TODAY, I ACHIEVED _____

_____

_____

_____

AND I LEARNED _____

_____

_____

_____

RESET

OVERALL, TODAY, MY MENTAL "RESET" SCORE WAS:

◯   ◯   ◯   ◯   ◯

1   2   3   4   5

REGRESSION   *PROGRESSION*

YOU CAN DO IT ALL
Tips from My Post-Pandemic Journey

Update

Before concluding this project with you, I want to give you some tips on how you can do it all, have it all, and own it all. Since the pandemic, I've been so busy with the Mrs. American Pageant, being a mom of two amazing little boys, being the wife of the most incredible husband in the world, and of course, starting up multiple businesses at once. "Dhomonique, how do you balance it all? How do you do all of that at once?" In this last section of my book, I'll show you how I do it all and give you tips on how you can optimize your success journey from start to finish.

I will share three powerful tips with you that you cannot do without if you want to sustain recurring and consistent success on media outlets and/or in your business or with your service/product. I am sharing this with you, not only so that you will succeed in everything you do, but that you will succeed to the *highest* level in everything you do. I do not mean that you will get your way all of the time, but I do mean that even if you run into a closed door, I am going to equip you with the tools and strategies of how you can work around the door, beat down the door, pry open the door, or even sometimes how to find the key to unlock the door. There is always a way forward; the key is paying attention to the signs around you and following those signs without fear.

Mrs. American

On March 26, 2021, I competed in the Mrs. American Pageant—a showcase of literally **the** most inspirational, incredible women in the nation. For ten days, I lived my dream. My experience was so wonderful. I am so grateful to have shared space with powerful women making real change, and they do it so gracefully. I came out of this experience with a top-15 placement, as well as the Most Photogenic Award. Even though I did not walk away with the crown I worked so hard for, I could not be more content and blessed in this moment. I am excited about my sister who won Mrs. American, and I am so thankful I had the experience of sharing the stage with such a jewel! I have the most supportive husband in the world, and my two boys are so wonderful.

This pageant was just one of many dynamics I've had to juggle. But when you think of a person juggling objects in their hands, you notice something: no matter how many objects the juggler has, he/she only ever has her hands on two or three at once. Everything else is up in the air. When we juggle multiple projects and/or lifestyles, we must bear this same concept in mind, and make peace with the fact that there will be at least one thing every day that our hands will not touch. Sometimes we have to forego the family time we want to accomplish our goals and sometimes, we have to give our goals a time out, so that we can fulfill our responsibilities. Just make sure that you just keep rotating your time: time management is everything. If you hold on to any one thing too long, everything could fall down.

My first tip to you is that you need to **master the art of switching hats**. You might be a parent, a spouse, an entrepreneur, and an employee all at the same time. Learn how to work within your schedule and manage your time appropriately among each lifestyle and/or project/endeavor. Juggle your goals and your responsibilities, understanding that something will miss your attention each day—just make sure that it is not the same thing missing your attention for too long. The moment you neglect something in your life, it will begin to fade away. Do not risk that. Failure does not deserve to be an option in your life.

My second tip to you is that you *have a resolute endurance*. CEO and founder of T. D. Jakes Enterprises © ™ Bishop T. D. Jakes said, "You can't be committed to the dream; you have to be committed to the process." Whatever dream lifestyle or goal you envision in your mind—keep it in the forefront of your mind to keep you motivated, but don't be so fixated on it that you despise the process to get there. In order to master the art of the juggle, you have to be resilient, persistent, consistent, and humble. You have to practice your pitch or message every day until you can say it in your sleep. You have to focus only on the things that will get you to your goals—everything else can wait. That means you need to trade in instant gratification for long-term manifestation. You cannot feed yourself out to your excuses/distractions and your goals at the same time. If you are saving up, lock down your spending. If you are changing your lifestyle, eliminate your indulgences; only give your energy to your goals.

You especially need to keep doing these things when you start to get tired of the process. That is the point to me, when the rubber really meets the road. Are you only interested in starting something, or are you truly committed to *achieving* something? I will not deceive you: this tip is hard to apply, because you aren't really applying it until it starts to hurt somewhere. But in my mind, you wouldn't have even looked at this book unless it was really in you to push past your limits. Sometimes, the top of the mountain looks further away when you are halfway there than when you start from the bottom; it's never the distance that makes the road ahead seem far—it's your energy. It doesn't matter if a finish line is only three feet in front of you; if you run out energy, the finish line will seem impossible.

What Makes Me Rise

I will be the first one to admit to you that I am *human*. I get tired. I lose motivation. I fall short of my goals sometimes. Sometimes, I even get distracted. But I can always redirect myself and get back where I need to be—but it's not because I'm so amazing! It's because I have my "why". What is my "why"? My "why" is what makes me rise when I fall down. My "why" is what disciplines me when I'm not motivated. My "why" is my husband and my two brilliant boys—Christian and Christopher. Being their mother and being my husband's wife gets me up early. They are why I stay up late every day, doing my God-given best to give my children the best opportunities and to support my husband to the fullest. I am sacrificing constantly for them because they fulfill me. I pour out my best every day because they replenish me. I work harder than anybody else because they drive me. They give me energy when I am tired. They push me to be better when I fall short of my goals.

My third tip to you is that you **need your "why"**. If you don't have a "why I *must* keep going" in your life, you will only end up asking yourself "why *should* I keep going?" Your why holds you accountable and keeps you grounded in your passion, especially in the middle of life's many throes. You **will** get tired. What is the "why" that will recharge you? You will not be motivated all of the time. What is the "why" that will keep you disciplined when your enthusiasm is exhausted? If you don't have that "why"—my friend—you are not ready to truly be successful. The moment you find that "why", you will always bring yourself back to what is important.

My Businesses, Your Success

Now that you have these three tips, I want to leave you with my services, which will be available for you to apply these tips as you make active strides toward your highest goals. I have been so busy—amidst everything else in my life—with starting and running my businesses. Media Mastery Now, The Luxure Group, The Right Method and Dhomonique Murphy Productions. MediaMasteryNow.com is a premiere media training agency that prepares and equips you with practical tools and strategies that you need to look and sound great telling compelling stories and land media opportunities, fast. It is—in essence—a master class for success, designed especially for two types of students: those who want to expand their media exposure into the hundreds of thousands and those who have a message, service, and/or product they want to take to the next level. I also people and organizations build stories behind their brands in order to reach a much larger audience and scale exponentially. I will let you in on a little secret. People do not buy products; they don't. People buy people and people buy passion and people and passion are based on a story. If you do not have a story, you are missing out on so many opportunities to increase your visibility. I help people every day build messages that are memorable and that matter. You can download my e-book: Speak Up: 5 Simple Hacks to Gain Confidence, Find Your Voice and Land Media

Opportunities by going to MediaMasteryNow.com Sign up on the homepage and your e-book will be delivered to your inbox. I offer lots of content, courses and networking opportunities to take you and your brand to the next level. Media Mastery Now doesn't just teach you how to be a "one hit wonder," it teaches and breaks down for you how you need to present yourself and the way you need to in order to secure deals and keep consistent, recurrent opportunities flowing in.

The Luxure Group is a Global modern-world public relations agency specializing in high-end mass media exposure for brands looking to make an impact. We have offices around the world and have one mission: To amplify bold brands. We place our clients on highly sought-after television, radio, magazine, newspaper and podcast platforms, and help with community and audience building, media relations, brand exposure, branding, and all aspects of public relations including crisis communications, online reputation management, products and event launches, media tours and so much more. Visit www. TheLuxureGroup.com to see how we can help you gain the visibility and credibility you deserve.

Come along with me inside the homes of some of the most influential people on the planet in The Right Method. You literally are 'Hanging with Dhom,' as I give you access like never before. Learn from the most successful people on the planet how they did it, why they did it and gain priceless insider information to transform your thinking and actions like never before. Visit TheRightMethod.com and sign up for updates today!

Dhomonique Murphy Productions helps CEOs, high-level execs and public figures amplify their personal and professional brands through award-winning cinematic video features. We build stories by way of video that are compelling, engaging and memorable. We help speakers build video reels that make them stand out, we help our clients gain massive exposure by building television reels from the ground up – even placing our clients on television in large markets of over a million households.

Be sure to visit Dhomonique.com so you can learn so much more about me, my brands and stay in contact. I would love the opportunity to help you *crush* your goals.

CONGRATULATIONS!
You Are Living Your Best Life

"You can't go back and change the beginning,
but you can start where you are and change
the ending." – C. S. Lewis

Recycle This Book

Although I am all about helping the environment, I mean something different by the above title. Whenever you recycle something, you use the same thing for another purpose. Likewise, I want you to take this book, ***start at the beginning again***, and use this book for another aspiration.

Paradigm shifting events will always happen, maybe not in the form of a pandemic, but they will happen in your life. As they happen, use this book to help you reset yourself, so that you can continue to achieve your aspirations in life. This way, you can always live your best life after a shaking event. You never have to fall victim to your circumstances. This does not always mean that you can change your circumstances or have control over them, but you do not have to be defined by their limitations.

Even though he was homeless and living in his car, Tyler Perry still wrote plays. Even after a job loss, failed marriage, and incessant nos from many publishers, J. K. Rowling still sought for someone who would publish her book series, "Harry Potter". Despite being bullied growing up, Bill Gates still developed his own software. You can do the same for yourself, but it requires that you reset yourself after every major paradigm-shifting event in your life.

Look at You

I just want to say—even if no one else has told you—I am so proud of you! Look at how far you have come. Look at the obstacles you overcame. Look at the lessons you learned. Look at the people you have helped. Look at the power you have gained. Look at how strong, incredible, and amazing you are! I especially want to congratulate you for choosing your best over everything else. You are so much more than what they said, or even what they didn't say. You have always got me in your corner. Now go out there and live your best life.

REFERENCES

Corey, M. S. (2014). *Groups, Process, and Practice* (9th ed.).
    Belmont, California: Cengage Learning.
Kuhn, T. (1996). *The Structure of Scientific Revolutions* (3rd ed.).
    Chicago, IL: University of Chicago Press.
Nardi, P. D. (2011). *Neuroscience of Personality: Brain Savvy
    Insights for All Types of People.* Los Angeles, CA:
    Radiance House.

ABOUT THE AUTHOR

Dhomonique is a 3x Emmy Award Winning TV Personality, Professional Speaker, Masterful Storyteller and one of the most sought-after media trainers in the world. She has trained professionals around the world on 6 of the 7 continents. She was named "Most Photogenic" at Mrs. America(n) 2021 and was crowned Mrs. Virginia American 2020. Dhomonique has appeared on stages across the nation and has been featured on The Steve Harvey Show, FOX, ABC, NBC, HSN, CBS and countless radio, print, and local television platforms. She is also the recipient of the coveted 2020 Salute to Excellence Award from the National Association of Black Journalists—a nationally recognized award. Dhomonique is a published author of *RESET: Attitude is Everything, and RESET 2.*

TESTIMONIALS

"Dhomonique has been an amazing inspiration for me and many others across the world! It has been a phenomenal journey learning from an expert in her craft, both on the air and off! I have followed her career and accomplishments for years and have seen her commitment to understanding the importance of people. She also understands the importance of connecting with people through development, training, and resources. No matter where her talents take her, I am always able to count on her to provide some nuggets of wisdom to continue growing both personally and professionally! She has a template for success as she continues to willingly share her knowledge, wisdom, and passion for excellence with me! If you are looking to catapult yourself or your business to new heights of success, Dhomonique can help navigate that journey to a notable victory!"

-Audra Jones, President/CEO, Krystal Klear Communications

"Dhomonique is the world's most inspiring and gifted interviewer." -Mitzi Perdue, Speaker and World Thought Leader

"You are working now with Dhomonique, who is one of the most inspiring and most helpful people that you'll ever work with, and if you follow her ideas over and over again, you will accomplish more in the weeks and months ahead than you may have ever accomplished in your whole lifetime." - Brian Tracy, World-Renowned Leadership Authority

---

"Dhomonique provided me with the inspiration and skills to successfully prepare for my first TV interview. Because of her expertise and talent, I am now a more effective public speaker, and my media interactions are with comfort and ease. I am grateful to Dhomonique, because I finally have the strategies to handle press engagements with confidence and finesse. She is definitely an expert in her field who can make anyone shine." - Darla Edwards, President/CEO, Successful Innovations

---

"You gotta follow her. Stay close to her and see everything that she does, because it's transformational." -Mitch Axelrod, #1 Bestselling Author, Speaker, Strategist-IP

"I worked with Dhomonique for several years in my second TV market. She was a force in the newsroom as a main anchor, as well as a go-to mentor for any situation life threw my way. She helped me when it came to my on-air presence, storytelling, and connections in the business. On top of that, and more importantly, she was there for me personally whenever I needed her. At a point in my life when I just needed someone to listen,

she sat with me in the conference room before work any time I needed her. Not only does she give sound advice, but she always made herself available, dropping whatever she was doing, to help others. When we worked together, she did all of this out of the kindness of her heart...I can only imagine what she'd be like doing this as a full-time job." -Melissa Stern, Television Reporter, CBS46, Atlanta

---

"I am an advocate for doing things the right way. I didn't really know what all that meant until I met Dhomonique Murphy, and let me tell you something: If you've been doing it the wrong way, if you're suffering or struggling, she's got insight information and access to some of the most amazing people." -Forbes Riley, Queen of Pitch, Celebrity TV Host

---

"Dhomonique is a wealth of valuable insight and provides such impactful key learnings in an easy to understand manner. What a pleasure!" - Linda Fisk, Co-Founder, LeadHERship Global

---

"Dhomonique Murphy is an amazing person. She is beautiful inside and out. Her positive energy is contagious. In [her] RESET book, it trains your mindset to be inspired to know that the sky is the limit! Thank you for being a role model for me and so many across the globe. Attitude is everything." - Felissa Johnson

"Dhomonique is phenomenal in EVERY way! From the moment I met Dhomonique, I was struck by her authenticity, humble nature, and warm spirit. She is engaging, and is a person who leads with her sincerity and compassion. I am inspired by Dhomonique's ability to embrace a broad audience and provide expertise in areas such as motivation/mindset, leadership, and accomplishing goals, in spite of obstacles. I first met Dhom at a women's event, where she was the keynote speaker. Her message resonated with me and all who attended, and although the room was full, it was as if she was talking directly to me. That personalized approach and message make Dhomonique stand out above the rest and my go-to for any speaking engagement. When hosting the roundtable event (Lifting Others While We Rise), my co-host and I selected Dhomonique to be our emcee. She exceeded every expectation and was the run-away hit of the event. She brought the same passion to her volunteer role that she does to her Emmy award-winning stories. It is that commitment to excellence that is easily noted and much appreciated. I admire Dhomonique in so many ways--as a mother and wife, entrepreneur and journalist." -Nicole Jacobs Silvey, Connection Coach, KC

"Dhomonique is a driven, hard-working, poised individual who knows her craft well, lifts others up, and puts professionalism first." - Kristin Volk, CEO and Marketing Director, Walter Haverfield, LLP

"I am in AWE of this amazing woman: full of life, generosity, wisdom, and class. She brings it all. Dhomonique is the epitome of what we all strive to be as far as leaders, influencers, and trailblazers in this world and in what we call everyday life. There are things we cannot teach, such as personality, charisma, and authenticity—Dhomonique has all three, plus the highest level of integrity and professionalism you won't find very often. I hold her in the highest regards." -Orly Amor, International Speaker, Author, Trainer

"Dhomonique's RESET book and presentation is a game-changer for all teachers! Her delivery, engagement, passion, and positivity allowed her to connect with my students on many levels. Dhomonique inspired and motivated them to set personal and professional goals by using the RESET book to document their progress...a valuable tool that they can use throughout their lives." - Sara Lewis, Teacher, SiaTech

"Dhomonique has helped me to become healthy physically and mentally. She's always selfless and hospitable at all times. I enjoy her energy and her willingness to fully complete tasks. She's always very supportive and relatable. One thing I will forever hold on to is her eagerness to nurture. I am grateful to have met her—she has helped change my outlook on the world." -Michelle Sailes, CEO, Halo Crowning Glory

My life changed working with Dhomonique. My very first session was just like, "Wow!" It was only two hours, but she was able to take my story and turn it into something that moves people! When I had the opportunity to tell my story, people were clapping and just amazed--mind you, at this point, I wasn't even finished with sessions with Dhomonique! I almost cried! This has never happened to me before! Then, they asked me to reach out to them again to have my story put in a magazine. It wasn't about my story; it was about how my story was moving people. Dhomonique will work with you, she will hear you, and she will encourage you. She is so authentic and inspirational! Thank you, Dhomonique, for creating a safe space for me! I'm looking forward to continuing to work with you! – Clemence Famen

---

I was on a platform called the Clubhouse, and my pitch was nowhere near ready. But after one half-hour coaching session with Dhomonique, she really taught me vocabulary and speaking skills you would never even think of in order to grab your audience's attention, and now, I'm more ready than ever! – Mahamed

---

Dhomonique, thank you so much for the past two weeks! I've increased my clientele 25 percent, I found different ways to reach my clients, and I felt like a more confident me. I couldn't have asked for a better business coach! Thank you! - Kawanis Ellison